Wiccan Mysticism and Spirituality

Journeying into the Mystical Realm: Exploring Wiccan Spirituality and Mysticism

Felix Roberts

Table of Contents

INTRODUCTION

Welcome to "Wiccan Mysticism and Spirituality: Journeying into the Mystical Realm Exploring Wiccan Spirituality and Mysticism." This book is a gateway to understanding Wicca's rich and profound tradition, offering both newcomers and seasoned practitioners a deeper look into its mystical aspects.

Wicca, often misunderstood, is a modern pagan witchcraft religion with ancient roots that honors nature, the cycles of the Earth, and the divine in many forms. At its heart, Wicca is a profoundly spiritual path that encourages personal growth, harmony with nature, and a profound connection with the mystical forces of the universe. This book delves into the core beliefs, practices, and rituals that define Wiccan spirituality, providing a comprehensive guide to its mysterious traditions.

Our journey begins with an exploration of Wicca's historical foundations and core principles, setting the stage for a deeper understanding of its spiritual practices. We will then explore the tools, rituals, and ceremonies that form the backbone of Wiccan worship. As we go farther, we will explore more complex mystical techniques like dream work, shadow work, and astral travel, providing methods and insights for individuals looking to develop their spiritual practice.

Whether you are a solitary practitioner or part of a coven, this book aims to be a trusted companion on your spiritual journey. May it inspire and guide you as you explore Wiccan spirituality's enchanting and mystical realms. Blessed be.

CHAPTER I

Wiccan Mysticism and Spirituality

Definition of Wiccan Mysticism

At its core, Wiccan mysticism is the spiritual and esoteric heart of the Wiccan faith, embracing a profound connection to the divine, nature, and the mysteries of the universe. Unlike Wicca's more exoteric, ritualistic aspects, mysticism delves into the inner, personal experiences of the divine, seeking to understand and unify with the spiritual forces that govern the cosmos. This path of mysticism within Wicca emphasizes direct, personal experiences of the sacred, transcending traditional religious dogma and focusing on an intimate relationship with the divine.

Wicca, as a modern pagan religion, is deeply rooted in ancient practices that honor the cycles of nature and the immanent presence of the divine in all things. Wiccan mysticism, therefore, is inherently tied to nature. Practitioners see the natural world as a living, breathing manifestation of sacred energy. This perspective fosters a deep reverence for the earth and all its creatures, encouraging a harmonious and respectful interaction with the environment. Mystical experiences often arise from communion with nature, where the veil between the mundane and the sacred is thin, allowing practitioners to perceive the divine essence in the world around them.

Central to Wiccan mysticism is immanence—the belief that the divine is present and active within the material world and each individual. This contrasts transcendence, where the sacred is seen as distant and separate from the physical realm. In Wiccan practice, the holy is not confined to a distant heaven but is intertwined with every aspect of existence. This immanent view of divinity means that mystical experiences can occur in everyday life, in the quiet moments of contemplation, in the beauty of a sunset, or the sacred space of a ritual circle.

Wiccan mysticism often involves techniques designed to heighten awareness and facilitate direct encounters with the divine. Meditation is crucial, helping to quiet the mind and open the heart to spiritual insights. Through meditation, practitioners can connect with their inner selves and the divine presence within, achieving heightened consciousness and inner peace. Visualization is another essential technique to create vivid mental images that can be gateways to mystical experiences. By visualizing sacred symbols, deities, or natural scenes, Wiccans can enter altered states of consciousness where they can communicate with the divine and receive guidance and inspiration.

Rituals and ceremonies are essential in Wiccan mysticism because they provide an organized way to invoke the divine and promote mystical experiences. These rituals often involve casting a sacred circle, calling upon the elements, and invoking deities. Within the protected space of the circle, practitioners can focus their intentions and energies, opening themselves to the presence and power of the divine. Using symbols, chants, and gestures in rituals helps create a sacred atmosphere conducive to mystical experiences.

One of the most profound aspects of Wiccan mysticism is the concept of the "Great Mystery," the ultimate source of all creation and the unifying force behind the universe. This mystery is often personified as the Goddess and the God, representing the feminine and masculine aspects of the divine. However, Wiccan mysticism acknowledges that the true nature of the holy is beyond human comprehension, existing as a profound mystery that can be approached but never fully understood. This sense of mystery encourages a humble and open-minded approach to spirituality, where seekers continually learn and evolve in their understanding of the divine.

Another essential element of Wiccan mysticism is the idea of personal transformation. Through mystical practices, individuals seek to transcend their ordinary consciousness and connect with their higher selves, achieving greater wisdom, compassion, and spiritual insight. This transformative process is often symbolized by the Wheel of the Year, a cycle of seasonal festivals that reflect the cycles of nature and the stages of spiritual growth. By aligning themselves with these natural cycles, Wiccans believe they can harmonize their inner lives with the rhythms of the cosmos, fostering personal and spiritual development.

Wiccan mysticism also emphasizes the interconnectedness of all life. This holistic view sees all beings as part of a vast web of existence, where each individual is connected to every other part of creation. This interconnectedness fosters a sense of unity and compassion, encouraging practitioners to live in harmony with others and the natural world. Mystical experiences often reinforce this sense of unity, providing profound insights into the interconnected nature of all things.

In summary, Wiccan mysticism is a deeply personal and experiential aspect of Wiccan spirituality that seeks to connect with the divine presence in all things. It emphasizes the inherent nature of the sacred, the sacredness of nature, and the transformative power of mystical practices. Wiccans strive to achieve a profound understanding and unity with the spiritual forces that govern the universe through meditation, visualization, ritual, and a humble approach to the Great Mystery. This path of mysticism offers a rich and fulfilling journey of spiritual growth, personal transformation, and a deeper connection with the divine.

Purpose and Scope of the Book

The purpose of " Wiccan Mysticism and Spirituality: Journeying into the Mystical Realm Exploring Wiccan Spirituality and Mysticism" is to provide a comprehensive and insightful exploration of Wiccan spirituality, focusing on its mystical aspects. This book is designed to guide both novices and experienced practitioners who seek to deepen their understanding of Wicca and enhance their spiritual practice. During this journey, readers will receive a solid foundation in the core ideas of Wicca, along with useful tools and methods for exploring the mystical aspects of this path.

The book aims to demystify Wicca for those unfamiliar with the tradition, addressing common misconceptions and providing a clear, accurate depiction of its beliefs and practices. Wicca is often misunderstood and misrepresented in mainstream culture, and this book seeks to present an authentic view grounded in historical context and contemporary practice. By offering a balanced and respectful portrayal, the book hopes to foster greater acceptance and understanding of Wicca as a legitimate spiritual path.

This book serves as an introductory guide for beginners, offering a structured and accessible way to learn about Wiccan spirituality. It covers the essential elements of Wicca, including its history, core beliefs, and ritual practices. This foundational knowledge is crucial for anyone new to the path, providing the context and framework to embark on a personal spiritual journey. The book also includes practical advice on how to set up an altar, perform basic rituals, and incorporate Wiccan principles into daily life.

For more advanced practitioners, the book delves into Wiccan mysticism's more profound, more esoteric aspects. It explores advanced practices such as astral travel, dream work, and shadow work, offering detailed guidance on incorporating these techniques into one's spiritual practice. The book looks at these mystical practices to assist seasoned Wiccans in reaching higher levels of awareness and strengthening their relationship with the divine. It also provides insights into personalizing and enhancing one's rituals, making them more powerful and meaningful.

Another essential purpose of the book is to emphasize the relevance of Wiccan spirituality in contemporary life. Wicca offers a path back to a more harmonious and holistic way of living in a world that often feels disconnected from nature and spirituality. The book highlights how Wiccan principles can be applied to modern challenges, such as environmental issues, personal wellness, and community building. By showing how Wicca can be a source of guidance and support in everyday life, the book aims to make the tradition more accessible and appealing to a broader audience.

The book is a wide range of issues relating to Wiccan spirituality and mysticism, and its broad and deep reach.

It begins with a thorough exploration of Wicca's historical and cultural origins, providing a solid foundation for understanding its evolution and contemporary practice. From there, it examines Wicca's core beliefs and principles, such as the Wiccan Rede, the Threefold Law, and the significance of the elements and the Wheel of the Year.

The book then transitions into practical guidance on Wiccan rituals and ceremonies, offering step-by-step instructions for creating sacred space, casting circles, and performing various types of rituals. It also covers the use of magical tools and correspondences, helping readers understand how to incorporate these elements effectively into their practice. This practical section is designed to be user-friendly and accessible, providing clear instructions and tips for solitary practitioners and those working within a coven.

As the book progresses, it delves into the mystical aspects of Wiccan spirituality, exploring topics such as meditation, visualization, and divination. It provides techniques for developing intuitive abilities and connecting with the divine through various forms of divination, such as tarot, runes, and scrying. The book also examines the role of deities in Wiccan practice, offering insights into building relationships with the divine and incorporating deity work into rituals and daily life.

In its advanced sections, the book explores more esoteric practices such as astral travel, dream work, and shadow work. These chapters provide detailed guidance on safely and effectively engaging in these practices, offering tips for preparation, execution, and integration. The goal is to help readers achieve profound spiritual experiences and personal transformation, deepening their connection with the divine and understanding of themselves.

Ultimately, the purpose and scope of "Wiccan Mysticism and Spirituality: Journeying into the Mystical Realm

Exploring Wiccan Spirituality and Mysticism" is to serve as a comprehensive guide to Wiccan spirituality, offering foundational knowledge and advanced practices. It aims to demystify Wicca, provide practical tools for spiritual growth, and highlight the relevance of Wiccan principles in contemporary life. Whether you are a curious newcomer or an experienced practitioner, this book is meant to guide and encourage you as you travel the spiritual path, assisting you in discovering and embracing the ethereal world of Wiccan spirituality.

Brief History of Wicca

Wicca is a modern pagan religion that has captured the imagination of many with its rich blend of ancient traditions, reverence for nature, and focus on personal spirituality. Despite its contemporary emergence, Wicca draws deeply from historical sources, making it a fascinating amalgamation of old and new. Understanding the brief history of Wicca involves tracing its roots back to ancient pagan practices, examining its development in the mid-20th century, and exploring its evolution into the diverse and dynamic spiritual path it is today.

The term "Wicca" itself is derived from the Old English word "wicca" (pronounced "witch-a"), meaning "witch," and reflects a revival of pre-Christian pagan practices. Ancient paganism, particularly the nature-based religions of Europe, forms the bedrock of Wiccan traditions. These early religions were characterized by polytheism, animism, and the celebration of seasonal festivals, all elements that are integral to modern Wicca. The reverence for nature, the cycles of the moon and sun, and the veneration of various deities can be traced back to these ancient roots.

The formalization of Wicca as a distinct religion began in the early 20th century, mainly due to the work of Gerald

Gardner, often considered the father of modern Wicca. Gardner, an Englishman with a deep interest in esotericism and the occult, claimed to have been initiated into a surviving coven of witches in 1939. This coven, which he called the New Forest Coven, allegedly preserved ancient pagan practices that had been passed down through generations. While the historical accuracy of Gardner's claims is debated, his influence on Wicca is undeniable.

In 1954, Gardner published "Witchcraft Today" , a book that brought Wicca to the public's attention. He presented Wicca as a legitimate, surviving form of pre-Christian paganism and outlined its rituals, beliefs, and practices. Gardner's writings were instrumental in shaping the early form of Wicca, which became known as Gardnerian Wicca. This tradition emphasized worshiping a God and Goddess, using ritual tools, and celebrating the eight Sabbats of the Wheel of the Year. Gardnerian Wicca also introduced the concept of covens, small groups of practitioners who meet regularly for rituals and ceremonies.

Gardner's work sparked a resurgence of interest in witchcraft and paganism, forming various other Wiccan traditions. One of the most notable is Alexandrian Wicca, founded by Alex Sanders in the 1960s. Alexandrian Wicca closely resembles Gardnerian Wicca but incorporates additional ceremonial elements and emphasizes magic and the mystical aspects of the craft. Other traditions, such as Seax-Wica, founded by Raymond Buckland, and Dianic Wicca, which focuses on feminist spirituality and the worship of the Goddess, further diversified the Wiccan landscape.

The 1970s and 1980s saw Wicca gain increasing visibility and acceptance, particularly in the United States and the United Kingdom. The publication of influential books marked this period, the establishment of Wiccan organizations, and the growing presence of Wiccan voices in the broader pagan community. Authors like Doreen Valiente, Scott Cunningham, and Starhawk contributed significantly to Wiccan literature, making the practices and philosophies of Wicca more accessible to a broader audience. The rise of the internet in the late 20th century further accelerated the spread of Wiccan ideas and facilitated the formation of online communities.

Wicca's appeal lies in its flexibility and emphasis on personal experience. Unlike many organized religions, Wicca does not have a central authority or a fixed doctrine. That allows practitioners to tailor their practice to their needs and beliefs, drawing from various sources and traditions. Wicca's inclusive and eclectic nature has contributed to its rapid growth and diversification. Today, Wicca encompasses a broad spectrum of beliefs and practices, from traditional coven-based rituals to solitary eclectic practices that incorporate elements of other spiritual paths.

Despite its relatively recent origins, Wicca has become a significant and enduring spiritual movement. Its emphasis on nature, personal spirituality, and the divine feminine resonates with many people seeking an alternative to mainstream religious traditions. Wicca's focus on environmentalism and social justice also aligns with contemporary concerns, making it relevant today. As Wicca continues to evolve, it remains rooted in the ancient wisdom of its pagan ancestors while adapting to the needs and aspirations of modern practitioners.

In summary, Wicca's history is a story of revival, adaptation, and growth. From its roots in ancient paganism to its formalization by Gerald Gardner and subsequent diversification, Wicca has emerged as a vibrant and dynamic spiritual path. Its journey reflects a broader trend of reawakening interest in nature-based spirituality and the search for personal, meaningful connections with the divine. Wicca offers a distinctive fusion of tradition and innovation, looking to the future while taking inspiration from the past as it develops further.

CHAPTER II

Origins and Evolution of Wicca

Historical Roots and Influences

Wicca is a contemporary pagan religion that has drawn much attention because of its emphasis on individual spirituality, appreciation for the natural world, and rich fusion of historical customs. Even though it emerged in the modern era, Wicca draws extensively from the past, creating an intriguing fusion of the ancient and the new. Comprehending the brief history of Wicca entails tracing its origins to prehistoric paganism, analyzing its growth in the middle of the 20th century, and investigating its transformation into the multifaceted and dynamic spiritual path it is today.

Originating from the Old English word "Wicca" (pronounced "witch-a"), which means "witch," the term "Wicca" itself refers to a resurgence of pre-Christian paganism. Wiccan traditions are rooted in ancient paganism, especially the nature-based faiths of Europe. The celebration of seasonal festivals, animism, and polytheism that typified these ancient religions are all essential components of contemporary Wicca. These ancient origins can be found in the respect for nature, the cycles of the sun and moon, and the adoration of many deities.

The early 20th century saw the formalization of Wicca as a separate religion, partly because of Gerald Gardner's contributions. Gardner is frequently referred to as the founder of contemporary Wicca. In 1939, Gardner—an Englishman with a keen interest in occultism and esotericism—said he had been initiated into a coven of witches that was still active. He dubbed this coven the

New Forest Coven, and it was said to have retained age-old pagan rituals that had been handed down through the centuries. Although there is disagreement regarding Gardner's historical authenticity, there is no denying his influence on Wicca.

Gardner's book " Witchcraft Today," released in 1954, became well-known and popularized Wicca. He described Wicca's rites, beliefs, and practices and presented it as a valid example of pre-Christian paganism. Gardner's teachings greatly influenced the early style of Wicca, known as Gardnerian Wicca. This tradition strongly emphasized celebrating the eight Sabbaths of the Wheel of the Year, using ritual equipment, and worshiping a god and goddess. The notion of covens—small gatherings of practitioners who get together frequently for rites and ceremonies—was also introduced by Gardnerian Wicca.

Gardner's writings spurred a revival of interest in paganism and witchcraft, which gave rise to other Wiccan traditions. The most well-known is Alexandrian Wicca, established in the 1960s by Alex Sanders. While Gardnerian Wicca and Alexandrian Wicca are similar, Alexandrian Wicca emphasizes magic and the mystical components of the craft more and adds more ceremonial elements. The Wiccan landscape was further expanded by other traditions, including Seax-Wica, which Raymond

Buckland developed, and Dianic Wicca, which emphasizes female spirituality and Goddess worship.

Wicca rose in popularity and acceptance in the US and the UK during the 1970s and 1980s. Essential books were published during this time, Wiccan organizations were founded, and Wiccan voices became more prevalent in the larger pagan world. Wiccan literature was greatly influenced by writers such as Doreen Valiente, Scott Cunningham, and Starhawk, who helped popularize Wicca's practices and ideas. The internet's emergence further aided the development of online groups and the dissemination of Wiccan beliefs in the late 20th century.

Wicca's emphasis on personal experience and flexibility makes it appealing. Compared to many other structured religions, Wicca needs a central body and a set doctrine. This enables practitioners to draw from various sources and traditions and customize their work to suit their needs and beliefs. Wicca's inclusive and eclectic character has aided in its explosive expansion and diversity. Wicca today includes a wide range of beliefs and activities, from customs centered around covens to solo eclectic rituals that blend aspects of several spiritual paths.

Even though Wicca is a relatively new spiritual movement, it has grown influential and long-lasting. Many people looking for an alternative to mainstream religious traditions find resonance in its emphasis on nature, individual spirituality, and the divine feminine. Wicca is still relevant in the modern world because of its focus on social justice and ecology. While adjusting to the requirements and goals of contemporary practitioners, Wicca maintains its foundation in the age-old knowledge of its pagan forebears.

In conclusion, the history of Wicca is a tale of growth, adaptation, and resurgence. From its roots in ancient paganism to its formalization by Gerald Gardner and subsequent diversification, Wicca has developed into a vigorous and active spiritual path. Its voyage indicates a more significant trend of resurging interest in spirituality rooted in nature and pursuing genuine, intimate relationships with the supernatural. Wicca offers a distinctive fusion of tradition and innovation, looking to the future while taking inspiration from the past as it develops.

Key Figures in Wiccan History

The formation and evolution of Wicca have been affected by the contributions of various influential persons throughout its history. These people, through their publications, teachings, and personal practices, have been instrumental in popularizing and establishing Wicca as a legitimate spiritual path. However, there are many influential Wiccan historical individuals, a few stand out for their innovative work and enduring influence.

Gerald Gardner, recognized for formalizing and popularizing Wicca in the middle of the 20th century, is frequently called the founder of contemporary Wicca. An anthropologist by training and an avid occultist, Englishman Gardner claimed in the 1930s to have been initiated into a witchcraft coven in the New Forest region of England. Gardner wrote other books, such as "Witchcraft Today" (1954) and "The Meaning of Witchcraft" (1959), based on his studies and experiences. In these works, he described Wicca as a kind of pre-Christian pagan witchcraft that has survived. The foundation of the first official Wicca tradition, Gardnerian Wicca, consisted of Gardner's initiation rites, rituals, and organizational structures.

Another important person in the history of the faith is Doreen Valiente, frequently described as the mother of modern Wicca. Gerald Gardner welcomed British poet and author Valiente into Gardnerian Wicca, and Valiente played a major part in forming and growing the tradition. She made significant contributions to the theology, rites, and liturgy of Gardnerian Wicca, aiding in codifying and improving its practices. Because of Valiente's lyrical talents, many of the rites and invocations utilized in Gardnerian Wicca have a sense of beauty and reverence. In addition, she authored other publications on Wicca, such as "Witchcraft for Tomorrow" (1978), which contributed to the religion's increased popularity.

During the 1960s and 1970s, Alex Sanders, also referred to as the "King of the Witches," was a well-known figure in the British Wiccan community. Sanders established his own Wicca lineage, known as Alexandrian Wicca, after claiming that his grandmother had initiated him into witchcraft. This was similar to Gardnerian Wicca but with more ceremonial components and a stronger focus on magical operations. Sanders' flamboyant demeanor and open rituals contributed to the increased awareness of Wicca, which has led to its increasing popularity in the UK and other countries.

Through his publications, English-born Wiccan author and practitioner Raymond Buckland significantly contributed to the introduction and popularization of Wicca in the United States. In the 1960s, Buckland received his first instruction in Gardnerian Wicca. He then established Seax-Wica, his tradition that modified Wiccan rituals to meet American practitioners' demands better. Among the many publications he authored about Wicca are "Witchcraft from the Inside" (1975) and "The Complete Book of Witchcraft" (1986), which have become must-reads for anybody wishing to practice Wicca. Buckland's work helped pave the road for Wicca's widespread acceptance and expansion in the United States by establishing it as a respectable and acceptable spiritual path.

Goddess-centered Wicca and ecofeminist spirituality have significantly benefited from the work of feminist author, activist, and priestess Starhawk. Her groundbreaking book "The Spiral Dance: A Rebirth of the Ancient Religion of the Great Goddess" (1979) introduced many people to the concepts of earth-based religion and feminine spirituality. Starhawk's emphasis on environmentalism, social justice, and goddess worship has drawn many people to Wicca as a spiritual path that reveres the divine feminine and the sanctity of nature.

These significant figures represent just a handful of the numerous people who have added to the rich tapestry of Wiccan history. Through their efforts, Wicca has become more widely known and accepted as a separate and dynamic spiritual tradition, encouraging countless practitioners to delve into its mysteries and accept its teachings. These characters act s beacons of guidance, reminding us of the timeless strength and beauty of this age-old yet perpetually rejuvenating path as Wicca develops and grows.

Evolution of Modern Wicca

The development of contemporary Wicca has been a dynamic and complex process spanning centuries, influenced by occultism, folklore, ancient pagan customs, and the innovative ideas of influential figures. From its modest origins as a clandestine underground movement to its rise to prominence as a respected and acknowledged religion, Wicca has experienced tremendous changes that mirror the shifting spiritual and cultural terrain of the contemporary world.

Fundamentally, Wicca has its roots in the pre-Christian, ancient pagan faiths of Europe. These religions recognized the natural cycles, worshipped various deities, and engaged in ritual magic. These early faiths influenced

Wicca's emphasis on natural spirituality, respect for the divine feminine, and ritual use to establish a connection with the holy. The advent of Christianity resulted in the loss or suppression of much of the knowledge of these antiquated rites. However, folk traditions, folklore, and oral lore preserved vestiges of pagan beliefs and behaviors.

Gerald Gardner, sometimes considered the father of contemporary Wicca, contributed to the formalization of Wicca as a separate religious movement in the middle of the 20th century. In the 1930s, Gardner—a British government servant and amateur anthropologist—said he was inducted into a coven of surviving witches in the New Forest area of England. Gardner wrote other works, such as "Witchcraft Today" (1954) and "The Meaning of Witchcraft" (1959), presenting Wicca as a respectable and historic kind of witchcraft based on his experiences and studies. The foundation of the first official Wicca tradition, Gardnerian Wicca, consisted of Gardner's initiation rites, rituals, and organizational structures.

Gardner was followed by several other notable individuals who also made significant contributions to the development and diversification of Wicca. Often recognized as the founder of contemporary Wicca, Doreen Valiente was instrumental in forming Gardnerian Wicca and developing its ritualistic and theological aspects. The "King of the Witches," Alex Sanders, established Alexandrian Wicca, primarily based on Gardnerian Wicca, with some added ceremonial components and a stronger focus on magical workings. In addition to bringing Wicca to the United States, Raymond Buckland established the Seax-Wica tradition, which modified Wiccan rituals to meet American practitioners' requirements better.

Wicca grew and changed during the second half of the 20th century and the first part of the 21st, impacted by technological advancements, culture, and society.

Traditions like Dianic Wicca, which concentrates solely on Goddess worship, were inspired by the feminist movement of the 1970s, which sparked a resurgence of interest in Goddess worship and the divine feminine within Wicca. Concerns about climate change and the environmental movement's growth have also impacted Wicca, inspiring many practitioners to embrace eco-spiritual practices and promote environmental stewardship.

The introduction of the internet has assisted the global expansion of Wicca, allowing practitioners to interact, share resources, and build virtual communities. Wiccans can share ideas, ask questions, plan events, and communicate through online forums, social media groups, and websites. The advent of multiple Wicca-related publications, blogs, and online courses has also occurred in this digital era, increasing the availability of information and resources.

Nowadays, Wicca has a thriving global community of practitioners and is acknowledged as a valid and respectable religion. It includes a broad spectrum of ideas, customs, and rituals, ranging from eclectic solo practices drawn from many sources to traditional Wicca centered around covens. The fundamental tenets of Wicca—respect for nature, celebration of the divine, and the quest for spiritual and personal development—remain accurate even as it develops and adapts to the needs and goals of its adherents.

In summary, the development of contemporary Wicca is evidence of the flexibility and tenacity of old spiritual practices in the face of modernity. Wicca has embraced innovation and diversity while staying faithful to its roots, having emerged from old pagan religions and formalized in the middle of the 20th century. Its growth has continued into the digital age. As it develops, Wicca offers a route of spiritual inquiry, self-determination, and sacred connection that appeals to seekers everywhere.

CHAPTER III

Core Beliefs and Principles

The Wiccan Rede

A collection of fundamental ideas and precepts that direct adherents on their spiritual path are central to Wiccan spirituality. The Wiccan Rede is an essential and well-known ethical code that summarizes the core of Wiccan philosophy and morals. It is a straightforward yet profound code. A common Wiccan proverb is "An it harm none, do what ye will," highlighting the value of living in peace with oneself, others, and the environment. This idea acknowledges the interdependence of all living things and people's need to act with compassion and mindfulness in their words, deeds, and thoughts.

The law of cause and effect, often known as the Threefold Law or the Law of Return, and the concept of personal accountability are the foundational ideas of the Wiccan Rede. This idea states that a person will receive three times back the energy or intention they send out into the universe. This knowledge emphasizes the value of acting morally and being aware of the effects of one's actions. By upholding the Wiccan Rede, Wiccans aim to develop a sense of awareness and responsibility in their relationships with people and the environment.

The Wiccan Rede is not meant to be a strict code of conduct but rather to provide a foundation for moral behavior. It urges people to use their own discretion and judgment to decide which behaviors are consistent with their goals and ideals. Wiccan spirituality, which enables people to create their spiritual paths based on their own experiences, beliefs, and insights, is known for its emphasis on personal autonomy and empowerment.

The Wiccan Rede also reflects a profound regard for the holiness of nature and the interdependence of all life. The Rede emphasizes the significance of living in harmony with the natural world and appreciating every living thing's intrinsic value and worth by calling for non-harm and respect for all beings. Wiccan spirituality, which sees the planet as sacred and works to preserve and celebrate its richness and beauty, is centered on this reverence for the natural world.

In addition to the Wiccan Rede, Wicca upholds several fundamental ideas and precepts that guide its spiritual activities and worldview. These beliefs include the idea that a divine force or energy, sometimes known as the Goddess and the God, permeates all of creation. Wiccans revere and worship this holy force in many ways, including as gods that stand in for the sun, moon, earth, and other natural elements. This polytheistic perspective expresses both a love for the holiness of all life and an understanding of the diversity and complexity of the divine.

Immanence, or the conviction that the divine is accessible and present in the physical universe and each human, is fundamental to Wiccan theology. The idea of transcendence, which holds that the sacred is distinct from the material world, opposes this worldview. According to Wicca, the divine is immanent and resides in the natural world and every living thing's heart and soul. This knowledge encourages practitioners to look within themselves and their environment for spiritual insight and direction because it creates a sense of closeness and connection with the divine.

The idea of polarity, or the awareness of complementary opposites in the universe and each person, is another fundamental tenet of Wicca. The dual qualities of the God and the Goddess, representing the feminine and male energies that permeate all of creation, are frequently used as symbols for this idea. Recognizing these polarities' connection and the dynamic balance they contribute to the world; Wiccans honor and appreciate them. This concept of polarity influences many facets of Wiccan ritual and symbolism, as well as the comprehension of life's cycles and seasonal changes.

In conclusion, the Wiccan Rede and the tenets that it is connected with form the basis of Wiccan spirituality, directing practitioners in their pursuit of spiritual and personal development. Wiccanism aims to develop a closer relationship with oneself, other people, and the universe's holy secrets by upholding non-harm ideals, individual responsibility, appreciation for nature, and the understanding of divine immanence and polarity. Wiccans defend the values of love, compassion, and respect for all beings and work toward living in harmony with the natural world by committing to these principles.

The Threefold Law

One of the central tenets of Wicca mysticism, known as the Threefold Law, regulates how one's actions will affect others. This idea, sometimes called the Law of Return, holds that an individual will get the energy or purpose they send out into the universe three times back. Put another way, whether a person's activities have beneficial or adverse effects, they will be amplified and reflected in them. The Threefold Law is founded on the principle of cause and effect, a significant element of Wiccan philosophy. It highlights the realization of the interdependence of all creatures and the influence that our words, deeds, and ideas have on the environment and ourselves.

The notion of karma, or cosmic justice, was fundamental to moral and ethical teachings in ancient spiritual traditions, where the Threefold Law started. Similarly, the Threefold Law in Wicca reminds practitioners of the value of moral conduct and individual accountability. It inspires people to think about their choices' effects and aim for balance and harmony in their relationships with other people and the environment.

The Threefold Law is a multifaceted law that influences human behavior and the larger patterns and movements of the cosmos. It is thought that the energy we release into the universe causes cosmic ripples that affect the things that happen in our lives and the conditions we find ourselves in. Wiccans apply the concepts of the Threefold Law to align themselves with the universe's natural rhythms and cycles, using the law of cause and effect to produce good things and spiritual development.

The Threefold Law is not a punishment-based philosophy, even though it is sometimes connected to cosmic justice and divine retribution concepts—instead, a rule of nature functions based on harmony and balance. Our activities produce energetic vibrations that impact our environment, much like a stone dropped into a pond will cause ripples to radiate in all directions. Understanding the interdependence of all things and the influence of our words, acts, and thoughts, we can deliberately seek positive change and more purposefully actualize our intentions.

The Threefold Law emphasizes the value of mindfulness and intentionality in our behavior as one of its main lessons. Understanding the energy, we emit into the universe allows us to accept accountability for our decisions and work toward harmonizing with the greater good. This entails practicing empathy and compassion for others and developing a sense of self-awareness and ethical discernment. We may minimize the possibility of unfavorable outcomes by ensuring that our actions are consistent with our values and intentions by acting with integrity and honesty.

The Wiccan community as a whole uses the Threefold Law as a moral compass and to guide individual behavior. Since we are all connected and our actions impact the awareness of the whole, it encourages practitioners to help and inspire one another. Wiccans can collaborate to bring about positive change and create a more peaceful and compassionate society by promoting a culture of love, cooperation, and respect for one another.

The Threefold Law is a central tenet of Wiccan theology that highlights the power of cause and effect and the interconnection of all beings. We can use the transforming power of the Threefold Law to bring about positive change in our lives and the world by acknowledging our actions' repercussions and trying to align ourselves with the highest good. We can better understand who we are and where we fit in the cosmos by practicing mindfulness, intentionality, and ethical discernment. This will eventually lead to more harmony, balance, and spiritual fulfillment.

The Elements: Earth, Air, Fire, Water, and Spirit

The elements are fundamental to Wiccan spirituality's knowledge of the natural world, ritual, and spiritual symbolism. The fundamental forces and energy that comprise the universe are represented by the building blocks of creation: Earth, Air, Fire, Water, and Spirit. Every element possesses distinct properties and connotations manifested in its symbolism, spiritual meaning, and correspondence.

Earth is frequently connected to the material world, stability and grounding. It stands for the material world and the observable facets of life, including the senses, the body, and the environment. The element of salt, the direction of the north, and the winter season are all associated with Earth. Earth is frequently called upon in ritual practice because it protects and anchors properties and connections to growth, fertility, and plenty.

Air is linked to intelligence, speech, and the mental domain. It symbolizes the element of air and the domain of consciousness, reason, and cognition. Air is associated with the element of feathers or incense, the east's direction, and the spring season. Air is associated with intellect, curiosity, and the force of spoken words; it is often summoned in ritual practice for its clarity, inspiration, and communication.

Fire is linked to the domain of will, passion, and metamorphosis. It stands for the element of fire and the ability of action and energy to transform. Summertime, the southerly orientation, and the element of candles or flames are all associated with fire. Fire is called upon in ritual practice for its vigor, intensity, and bravery, as well as for its connections to passion, creativity, and the capacity for change.

Emotion, intuition, and the subconscious are all connected to water. It stands for both the flexibility and adaptability of the emotional landscape and the water element. Water is associated with the element of bowls or cups, the season of fall, and the direction of the west. Water is called upon in ritual practice for its cleaning, healing, and cleansing properties, as well as its connections to intuition, empathy, and the secrets of the subconscious.

Spirit, the divine spark or essence that animates all living things, is frequently regarded as the fifth element. It ties us to the world of the sacred, the universe, and the intricate chain of existence beyond the physical sphere. Spirit is connected to the ether element, also known as akasha, which is thought to engulf and penetrate all other components. Spirit is called upon in ritual practice because of its relationship to the divine and because it is associated with wholeness, oneness, and the everlasting cycle of life, death, and rebirth.

The elements work together to create a sacred, intricate network of energy and meaning penetrating everything. Wiccans aim to gain a deeper connection to the divine and the profound mysteries of existence by comprehending and utilizing the elements to harmonious with natural cycles and rhythms of the cosmos. They aim to use the elements' transforming power to further their spiritual practice, realize their wishes, and become more aware of the larger cosmic forces through ritual practice, meditation, and contemplation.

CHAPTER IV

The Wheel of the Year

Sabbats and Esbats

In Wiccan spirituality, the Wheel of the Year is a holy calendar that denotes the passing of the seasons and the natural cycles. It consists of eight festivals, called Sabbats, that commemorate the equinoxes, solstices, and midpoints of each month; in addition, there are monthly events called Esbats that pay homage to the moon's phases. The Sabbats and Esbats work together to create a comprehensive framework for spiritual practice and ceremonial observance that offers chances for introspection, joy, and communion with the natural world.

The Greater Sabbats, commemorating the solstices and equinoxes, and the Lesser Sabbats, which honor the cross-quarter days between them, are the two primary groups into which the Sabbats are divided. Yule (Winter Solstice), Litha (Summer Solstice), Ostara (Spring Equinox), and Mabon (Autumn Equinox) are among the Greater Sabbats. These celebrations pay homage to the varying seasons and the natural world's genesis, development, fruition, and decline cycles. The Lesser Sabbats are Beltane, Lammas (also called Lughnasadh), Samhain, and Imbolc (sometimes called Candlemas). These celebrations are linked to themes of abundance, fertility, and commemoration of the ancestors, as well as agricultural and pastoral pursuits, including planting, harvesting, and caring for cattle.

Every Sabbat has a distinct symbolism, set of customs, and correspondences that represent the seasonal themes and energy connected to it. For instance, Yule observed on the Winter Solstice, commemorates the sun's rebirth and the longest night of the year. It's a time for reflection, rebirth, and building bonfires to fend off the gloom. Ostara observed on the Spring Equinox, symbolizes the equilibrium between day and night and the restoration of light and life to the land. It's a season for planting, fertility rites, and the joy of fresh starts. On the Summer Solstice, Litha is observed to commemorate the longest day of the year and the sun's zenith. It's a season of happiness, plenty, and harvest celebration. Mabon, which falls on the Autumn Equinox, heralds the start of the dark season and the second harvest. It's a season of giving thanks, introspection, and preparing for winter.

Wiccans celebrate monthly Esbats, which are celebrations of the moon's phases, in addition to the Sabbats. Although certain traditions may also commemorate the new moon or other lunar phases, esbats usually align with the full moon. Esbats offer chances for spellwork, meditation, divination, and strengthening spiritual links. They are frequently conducted outside, in gardens, or forested regions so that practitioners can connect with the earth's and the moon's inherent rhythms and energies.

In Wiccan spirituality, the moon's phases symbolize development, metamorphosis, and rebirth cycles. The new moon is connected to possibilities, fresh starts, and sowing seeds for future growth, but the full moon is connected to illumination, intuition, and the pinnacle of magical power. While the waning moon is connected to the release, banishing, and discarding of old patterns or energies, the waxing moon is linked to development, expansion, and the manifestation of intentions.

Wiccan spirituality generally uses the Wheel of the Year as a holy framework to direct practitioners in their relationship with the natural world and the life, death, and rebirth cycles. Wiccans aim to enhance their spiritual practice, establish a closer relationship with the divine, and harmonize with the earthly and cosmic rhythms and energies by commemorating Sabbats and Esbats. Wiccans celebrate life's richness and beauty by paying homage to the moon's phases and changing seasons. They also recognize the connection and connectivity of all species in the web of existence.

Significance and Rituals of Each Sabbat

In Wiccan spirituality, the Sabbats are holy celebrations corresponding with the Wheel of the Year, honoring the natural cycles and the varying seasons. Every Sabbat has its own meaning, symbolism, and ritual that correspond with the seasonal themes and energy. By keeping the Sabbats sacred, Wiccans want to develop a greater feeling of spiritual awareness and reverence for the divine, strengthen their bond with the natural world, and harmonize with the cycles of the earth and the universe.

Yule, observed on the Winter Solstice, commemorates the sun's rebirth and the year's longest night. It's a time for reflection, rebirth, and building bonfires to fend off the gloom. Candle lighting, Yule log burning, and food and drink sharing with close ones are a few examples of rituals. In addition, Yule is a time for divination, year-end introspection, and intention-setting.

Ostara observed on the Spring Equinox, symbolizes the equilibrium between day and night and the restoration of light and life to the land. It's a season for planting, fertility rites, and the joy of fresh starts. Planting seeds, decorating eggs, and picking wildflowers are a few examples of rituals. Ostara is a time to appreciate the harmony and balance of the natural world and for spiritual and physical cleaning and cleansing.

The celebration of Beltane, which falls on May 1st, heralds the arrival of summer and the height of natural resources and fertility. It is a season of delight, festivity, and respect for the holy marriage of the Goddess and the God. Weaving maypoles, building flower crowns, and starting bonfires are a few examples of rituals. In addition, Beltane is a time to celebrate life force energy and the love, passion, and creativity that permeate all of creation.

On the Summer Solstice, Litha is observed to commemorate the longest day of the year and the sun's zenith. It is a season of joy, plenty, and respect for the sun as the giver of life and light. Lighting bonfires, creating crafts with solar themes, and harvesting fruits and flowers are a few examples of rituals. Litha is a season of thanksgiving, introspection, and celebration of the abundant crops to come.

August 1st is Lammas, a holiday commemorating the first harvest and the start of the night. It's a season of giving thanks, plenty, and spreading blessings to others. Making corn dollies, preparing bread, and appreciating the soil for its abundance are a few examples of rituals. In addition to being a time for reflection, Lammas is also a time to prepare for the upcoming fall season.

Mabon, which falls on the Autumn Equinox, symbolizes the equinox, the second harvest, and the harmony of light and dark. It is a season of introspection, stability, and respect for the life-death-rebirth cycle. Crafts with a harvest theme, picking fruits and vegetables, and offering gratitude for the land's bounty are a few examples of rituals. Mabon is also a time to let go of things that no longer serve us and prepare for the reflective winter months.

In the Wiccan calendar, October 31st is Samhain, the start of the new year and the conclusion of the harvest season. It is a season of remembering and paying tribute to the ancestors, and the curtain between the realms is getting thinner. Lighting bonfires, presenting offerings to the spirits, and fortune-telling are a few examples of rituals.

Samhain is a time for reflection, welcoming new beginnings, and for letting go of the old.

The Sabbats are a precious and essential component of Wiccan spirituality, offering chances for introspection, festivity, and communion with the natural world. By keeping the Sabbats sacred and engaging in their customs, Wiccans aim to enhance their spiritual practice, establish a closer relationship with the divine, and harmonize with earthly and cosmic rhythms and energies. Wiccans recognize the interdependence and connectivity of all beings in the web of existence while also appreciating the beauty and diversity of life through the Sabbath celebrations.

Seasonal Cycles and Spiritual Significance

The varying seasons have great spiritual significance in the Wiccan faith because they symbolize the cyclical nature of life, death, and rebirth. The distinct energies, teachings, and growth possibilities that come with each season encourage practitioners to tune into the natural world's cycles and strengthen their relationship with the divine.

After winter's chilly, hibernating months, spring signifies the return of life and energy to the planet. It is a season of rebirth, rejuvenation, and the waking of the natural world from hibernation. Buds emerge on trees, the Earth starts to thrive with fresh growth, and flowers burst in a riot of color. Spring is connected to the element of Air, the direction of the East, and the themes of growth, new beginnings, and goal-pursuing in Wiccan spirituality. It's a time to make plans for the upcoming year and to sow seeds, literally and figuratively.

Summer is a season of plenty, energy, and maximum solar power. The soil is brimming with life, and the days are long and warm. Gardens are brimming with flowers and vegetables, while fields are thick with crops. Summer is linked to the themes of passion, creativity, and celebration in the Wiccan faith, the element of Fire, and the direction of the south. It's a time to celebrate the abundance and beauty of nature and have fun, laugh, and get together outside.

Autumn is a season of transition and change because the days get shorter and the temperature drops. Harvest time is when we gather and store the products of our labor in preparation for the upcoming winter. As the leaves change from green to gold, red, and orange, the land is blazing with color. Autumn is connected to the element of Water, the direction of the west, and the concepts of thankfulness, introspection, and letting go in Wiccan spirituality. It's a time to reflect on the previous year's benefits, let go of things that no longer serve us, and prepare for the reflective winter months.

Winter is a season of quiet, reflection, and darkness. Under a layer of snow, the land is inactive, and everything around us appears to be sleeping. It's a time for introspection, relaxation, and introspection. Winter is linked to the ideas of repose, rejuvenation, and rebirth in the Wiccan faith, as well as the element of Earth and the direction of the north. It is a moment to respect the cycles of life and death and tend to the dormant seeds of our fresh growth.

In the Wiccan faith, the seasonal cycles are very spiritually significant, offering chances for introspection, festivity, and spiritual communion. Practitioners aim to understand who they are and where they fit in the universe by tuning into the rhythms of the natural world. They revere the changing of the seasons as holy reminders of the life cycle's perpetual cycle of death and rebirth and the connectivity and interdependence of all creatures. Wiccans acknowledge the vast wisdom and mystery of the cosmos while celebrating the natural world's beauty and diversity via rites, ceremonies, and observances.

CHAPTER V

Sacred Space and Tools

Creating a Sacred Space

Sacred space is fundamental in Wiccan spirituality because it provides a setting for ritual, spiritual practice, and divine connection. By creating a holy place, practitioners can foster an atmosphere that supports spiritual development, self-reflection, and communication with sacred energy. This area functions as a haven where people can respect the sanctity of life, listen to the rhythms of the natural world, and ask the divine for direction and inspiration.

Setting an intention and practicing mindfulness are the first steps in creating a sacred environment. This entails dedicating time and effort to making an altar or particular space sacred for spiritual practice. Depending on the practitioner's tastes and available space, this area might be as basic as a room corner or as complex as a ritual chamber. Above all else, the place needs to be purified, cleaned, and given a sense of solemnity and reverence.

Purification is one of the most critical steps in building a sacred space. It clears the area of any unfavorable or stagnant energy and fosters an atmosphere of openness and clarity. Some examples of purification procedures are smudging with plants like sweetgrass or sage, misting with salt or holy water, or just imagining the area filled with pure, white light. By cleansing the area, practitioners establish a sense of safety and sanctity and a clean slate for spiritual activity.

After cleaning it, the area might be dedicated to a particular goal or deity. This could include praying and making invocations to the deity, calling upon the guardians of the four directions, or requesting the benefits of the elements. Through the act of consecrating the room, practitioners call on the divine to lead and guard them, creating a sacred container for their spiritual practice.

To further improve the spiritual atmosphere and allow communication with the divine forces, ritual instruments, and symbols are frequently used while constructing a sacred space, in addition to purification and consecration. Examples of these instruments are candles, incense, crystals, athames (ritual knives), chalices, pentacles, and other objects with individual energy and meaning. Practitioners can strengthen their intentions, concentrate their energies, and strengthen their relationship with the divine by introducing these tools into their holy space.

Following its creation and consecration, the holy area can be utilized for various spiritual rituals and activities, including spellwork, divination, meditation, and prayer. It can also be a location of peaceful reflection, self-examination, and connection with the natural world. Through consistent maintenance of their sacred space and spiritual activities conducted there, practitioners can deepen their relationship with the divine, develop a more profound sense of inner harmony and serenity, and harmonize with the universe's holy rhythms.

To sum up, constructing a sacred place is a potent and transforming ritual in Wiccan spirituality that enables practitioners to create a setting that supports spiritual development, divine connection, and personal transformation. Through purification, consecrating, and altar-setting, practitioners establish a sacred space where they can tune into the natural world's cycles, respect the sanctity of life, and ask the divine for direction and inspiration. Practitioners can strengthen their connection to the heavenly forces and improve the spiritual ambiance of their holy space by utilizing ritual tools and symbols.

Creating a sacred place is a continuous process of intention, mindfulness, and devotion that helps practitioners develop a stronger feeling of purpose, presence, and connection to the universe's sacred mysteries.

Altar Setup and Tools

In Wicca, the altar is the principal place of focus. It is a hallowed area for rituals, meditation, and divine communion. Depending on the practitioner's tastes and available space, altars might be intricate permanent structures or straightforward temporary setups. Whatever its shape, the altar is a physical manifestation of the energies and principles of sacrosanctity that are summoned and respected throughout Wiccan ceremonies.

Practitioners usually start by choosing a place that feels spiritually meaningful and energetically receptive when setting up an altar. This could be an outside area, a specific room or section, or even a transportable altar that can be put up and taken down as needed. Once a location has been selected, the altar can be decorated with a variety of implements, emblems, and offerings that represent the practitioner's spiritual journey and goals.

The choice and placement of ritual implements are some of the most critical aspects of altar preparation. The practitioners operate as channels for energy and intention, focusing and amplifying the practitioner's magical workings. Ahames, or ritual knives, chalices, candles, wands, and pentacles, are standard altar accessories. Each has a specific energy and symbolism of its own. Depending on the ritual or goal being worked with and personal preference, the arrangement of these tools on the altar may change.

For example, athames are used to direct energy and cast circles for ritual activity, related to the element of Fire and the masculine principle. On the other hand, Wands are employed in spellwork and invocation to channel and manipulate energy. They are connected to the element of Air and the feminine principle. Pentacles, which stand for the element of Earth, are used to consecrate and bless objects or areas. In contrast, chalices, which symbolize the element of Water, are used to hold offerings of Water or wine during libation rites.

Altars may be embellished with offerings and symbols that have spiritual or personal meaning for the practitioner in addition to ceremonial implements. These could be statues or pictures of gods, stones, plants, flowers, or other objects harmonizing with the practitioner's journey and objectives. By including these symbols and gifts in their altar arrangement, practitioners can strengthen their relationship with the divine, foster a sense of reverence and dedication, and create a holy space that represents their spiritual path.

Symmetry, balance, and symbolism are typically used as guidelines for arranging artifacts on the altar. To commemorate the sacred powers of the natural world, objects representing the four elements—Earth, Air, Fire, and Water—might be positioned in each of the four cardinal directions. A particular pattern of candles can symbolize the moon's phase, the moon's year, and the seas. It is possible to carefully arrange stones or crystals to form a grid for healing or manifestation work.

Setting up an altar is ultimately a very intimate and intuitive activity driven by the practitioner's objectives and personal relationship with the divine. The altar represents the practitioner's devotion and commitment to their spiritual path, regardless of its complexity or duration. Practitioners can emerge with a sense of inner peace and harmony, link themselves with the universe, and strengthen their relationship with the divine via ritual practice and meditation at the altar.

Consecration of Ritual Tools

Ritual items are given spiritual force, meaning, and aim through the sacred and ceremonial process of consecration, which is a part of Wiccan spirituality. Consecration is the process of bringing the tools into alignment with the practitioner's energy and intention and committing them to their intended magical or ritual usage. This technique is sometimes undertaken as part of a ritual or ceremony, during which the practitioner calls supernatural blessings and energies to sanctify and empower the equipment.

Consecrating ritual items purges them of undesirable or harmful energies and imbues them with empowering, uplifting energies consistent with the practitioner's aims. This increases the tools' efficacy in magical operations and ritual practice and forges a holy and peaceful bond between the practitioner and the tools. Additionally, consecration attunes the instruments to the frequencies of divine energy and guidance, thereby bringing forth the hidden spiritual potential within them.

Consecrating ritual objects can be done in various ways, from straightforward purification rites to complex ceremonial invocations. Cleaning the instruments with the four elements—Earth, Air, Fire, and Water—is a popular method for ridding them of bad or stagnant energy. This may involve dusting the tools with salt or holy water, passing them through the smoke of incense or sage, or exposing them to the light of a candle or the rays of the sun.

After being cleansed, the tools are usually charged with energy and intention through invocation, prayer, or visualization. To imbue the tools with divine power and guidance, one may invoke the blessings of the elements, deities, or other spiritual entities. The practitioner can also utilize their own energy and intention to give the instruments the characteristics they want them to have.

Specific tools may need special consecration ceremonies to fit their meaning and use. For example, an athame (ritual knife) may be consecrated with the elements of Fire and Air to imbue it with power and clarity of intention. In contrast, a chalice may be consecrated with the elements of Water and Earth to enhance its receptivity and grounding properties. Similarly, wands, crystals, and other ritual objects can be charged with particular intents and energies to improve their magical qualities.

To establish a sacred and peaceful atmosphere for magical operations and spiritual practice, practitioners can consecrate particular tools and their entire ritual space or altar. To sanctify the area and align it with the practitioner's aims, this may entail forming a circle, calling upon the guardians of the four directions, and requesting divine blessings and protection.

In the end, ritual instrument consecration is a highly private and sacred rite that symbolizes the practitioner's adoration, respect, and dedication to their spiritual journey. Practitioners can improve their magical abilities, strengthen their relationship with the divine, and establish a sacred and robust environment for spiritual development and transformation by carefully and intentionally consecrating their equipment. Practitioners can access the powerful energies of the divine and use them to materialize their intents and aspirations for their highest good through the rituals and ceremonies that utilize these consecrated items.

CHAPTER VI

Meditation and Visualization

Techniques for Meditation

In Wicca, meditation and visualization are two of the most effective methods for developing inner harmony and calm, strengthening one's spiritual consciousness, and strengthening one's relationship with the divine. These techniques include clearing the mind, concentrating attention, and achieving a profoundly relaxed and open condition of being. By adding meditation and visualization to their spiritual practice, practitioners can enhance their self-awareness, intention clarity, and alignment with the universe's sacred energies.

Mindfulness meditation, which entails focusing on the present moment and noticing the ideas, sensations, and emotions that arise without judgment or attachment, is one typical technique used in Wiccan meditation. This practice facilitates the development of a more transparent, more peaceful inner self and a more robust understanding of how everything is interconnected. There are ways to practice mindfulness meditation, including paying attention to your breath, repeating an affirmation or mantra, or just paying attention to your body's sensations.

Guided visualization is a further technique in Wiccan meditation that involves harnessing the power of the imagination to conjure vivid mental images that elicit particular sensations, emotions, and experiences. Traveling to hallowed places, speaking with spirit guides or gods, or investigating one's inner landscape are all possible scenarios in guided visualizations. Through this emotional and sensory engagement, practitioners can more powerfully access the transforming potential of the subconscious mind and materialize their wishes.

To enhance their meditation practice and achieve altered states of consciousness, Wiccans can also engage in several types of energy work and trance induction, apart from mindfulness meditation and guided imagery. Methods like energy grounding, chakra meditation, and trance dancing can help to expand awareness beyond the confines of the egoic mind and balance and harmonize the subtle energies of the body. These techniques help to engage and align the body, mind, and spirit for more profound spiritual activity, and they can be especially effective when paired with other types of meditation and visualization.

One of its main advantages is the capacity of meditation and visualization to strengthen one's relationship with the divine and enable direct communion with the universe's sacred forces. By engaging in these activities, practitioners can become open and receptive, which allows them to receive direction, insight, and inspiration from the spiritual world. Practitioners can tune into the subtle vibrations and messages of the divine, resulting in deep insights, healing, and transformation by stilling the mind and opening the heart.

Additionally, practitioners can focus their energy and intention more precisely and clearly by using meditation and visualization tools for spellwork and manifestation. By emotionally and vividly envisioning their wishes and aspirations, practitioners can enhance the strength of their intentions and align themselves with the forces of creation. Through meditation and visualization, one can effectively harness the creative power of the mind and spirit to create their greatest wishes and objectives, whether abundance, healing, or spiritual progress.

In conclusion, Wiccan spirituality uses meditation and visualization to strengthen spiritual awareness, foster inner harmony and tranquility, and strengthen one's relationship with the divine. By engaging in energy work, guided visualization, and mindfulness meditation, practitioners can enhance their awareness of themselves, their intentions, and their alignment with the universe's sacred energies. By integrating these methods into their spiritual routine, practitioners can harness the metamorphic potential of the mind and soul to materialize their most profound yearnings and ambitions in harmony with their ultimate welfare.

Guided Visualizations

Guided visualizations are a potent tool utilized in Wiccan spirituality to improve one's relationship with the divine, access inner wisdom, and actualize intentions with clarity and potency. A key component of these guided trips is using the imagination to conjure up vivid mental images that elicit particular emotions, sensations, and experiences. Through this kind of engagement with sensations and emotions, practitioners can access the subconscious mind's transforming ability and release its latent potential.

One of guided visualization's main advantages is its capacity to transcend the constraints of the conscious mind and reach higher states of consciousness and awareness. Practitioners can access the intuitive wisdom of the subconscious by stepping outside of the analytical mind and into a state of calm receptivity. This facilitates deeper healing and change, as well as the emergence of deeper insights, clarity, and guidance.

Through guided visualizations, practitioners can travel to hallowed places and communicate with gods, spirit guides, and other spiritual entities. These travels could take you to the astral plane, into the inner landscape of the psyche, or contact with the energy of nature. Practitioners can strengthen their relationship with the divine and gain direction, knowledge, and inspiration from the higher realms by partaking in these guided travels.

Another advantage is the capacity of guided visualizations to promote healing and transformation on all planes of existence—physical, emotional, mental, and spiritual—. By envisioning themselves as entire, healthy, and vibrant creatures, practitioners can activate the body's intrinsic healing potential and bring about remarkable transformations in awareness. Guided visualizations can also be used to release negative emotions, beliefs, and habits that no longer serve one's highest benefit, allowing for greater clarity, freedom, and empowerment to arise.

Using guided visualizations for manifestation and spellwork, practitioners can focus their energy and intention more precisely and clearly. By emotionally and vividly envisioning their wishes and aspirations, practitioners can enhance the strength of their intentions and align themselves with the forces of creation. Whether visualizing riches, love, or spiritual growth, guided visualizations are a tremendous technique for harnessing the creative force of the mind and spirit to manifest one's most significant wants and objectives.

In addition to their practical benefits, guided visualizations can be tremendously transformational and uplifting experiences on a personal and spiritual level. By partaking in these guided experiences, practitioners can acquire a more profound sense of self-awareness, inner serenity, and spiritual connection. They can also gain increased trust in their intuition, inventiveness, and ability to co-create their world harmoniously with their highest good.

Ultimately, guided visualizations are a versatile and powerful approach that can be employed for various reasons in Wiccan spirituality. Whether seeking guidance and inspiration from the divine, enabling healing and transformation, or manifesting goals and aspirations, guided visualizations offer a tremendous technique of harnessing the creative force of the mind and spirit to bring about positive change in one's life. Through regular practice and purpose, practitioners can uncover the hidden potentials inside and tap into the unlimited possibilities of the universe.

Incorporating Elemental Energies

The elements—Earth, Air, Fire, Water, and Spirit—are seen as the essential components of the cosmos in Wiccan spirituality, and each has unique attributes, powers, and symbolism. A key element of Wiccan ritual and magic is the integration of elemental energies, which enable practitioners to use the natural world's primordial powers to materialize their wishes, strengthen their bonds with the divine, and harmonize with the cycles of the cosmos.

Earth symbolizes the material and physical worlds and is linked to the traits of abundance, stability, and grounding. Using earth energy in spiritual practice can entail working with crystals, stones, herbs, or other natural objects. It can also involve grounding and earth-based rituals to establish a connection with the energy of the land.

Air symbolizes the mental and cognitive domains linked to intelligence, clarity, and communication. Some ways to incorporate Air energy into spiritual practice include breathwork, visualization, or meditation techniques that increase awareness, spark creativity, and improve attention and mental clarity.

Fire symbolizes the world of energy and vigor and is connected to passion, transformation, and action. Working with candles, bonfires, or other sources of flame, as well as partaking in rituals or practices that stimulate the energy of passion, inspiration, and creativity, are some ways to incorporate fire energy into spiritual practice.

Water symbolizes the domain of emotions and the subconscious mind and is connected to feelings, intuition, and healing. Working with water rituals, like bathing or swimming, and partaking in exercises that develop emotional awareness, intuition, and empathy are some ways to incorporate Water energy into spiritual practice.

Spirit is the fifth element, the divine essence that gives life to everything. It is the totality of existence that exists outside of the physical world. Including Spirit energy into spiritual practice can entail developing awe and regard for the sacredness of all life and establishing a connection with the divine through prayer, meditation, or ceremonial invocation.

Casting circles is a ritual to create a sacred and protected place for spiritual ceremonies and magical workings. It is a typical way to incorporate elemental forces into spiritual practice. The circle is usually divided into four quarters, with Spirit encircling the center. The quarters correlating to the elemental forces are Earth in the north, Air in the east, Fire in the south, and Water in the west.

Practitioners can unite with the natural forces and create a robust container for spiritual work by calling upon the blessings and protection of the elements and evoking their energies.

Practitioners may use particular elemental correspondences in their magical workings and rituals in addition to casting circles. For example, to increase the energy and intention of a specific element, they might employ herbs, stones, or colors related to that element. To invoke the blessings and attributes of the elements, they may also include elemental invocations, prayers, or chants in their ceremonies.

Incorporating elemental forces into spiritual practice is ultimately a potent and transforming means of strengthening one's relationship with the divine, the natural world, and oneself. Practitioners can develop a stronger sense of harmony, balance, and alignment in their lives and access the infinite potential and wisdom of the cosmos by intentionally interacting with the elemental forces of nature. Using consistent practice and deliberate desire, practitioners can utilize the elemental energies to actualize their goals, enhance their spiritual consciousness, and collaboratively build a world that aligns with their ultimate welfare.

CHAPTER VII

Rituals and Ceremonies

Structure of a Wiccan Ritual

Rituals and ceremonies are very important in Wicca. They provide practitioners with a chance to acknowledge the cycles of nature, commune with the divine, and use energy work and focused intention to actualize their goals. Some universal components and activities are usually included in most Wiccan ceremonies, even though the precise format may differ based on custom, ancestry, and individual preference.

One of the main elements of a Wiccan ceremony is the establishment of sacred space, which is frequently accomplished by casting a circle. The circle creates a safe and effective environment for ritual activity by acting as a container for magical energy, shielding the practitioners and the sacred area from outside influences. The circle can be physically drawn on the ground using stones, candles, or other objects. Alternatively, it can be imagined and energetically formed via purpose and vision.

Following the casting of the circle, the practitioners might invoke the powers of the five elements—Spirit, Air, Fire, Water, and Earth—to bless and sanctify the area. This can entail asking for the blessings of the elements, contacting their spirits or guardians, and making prayers or invocations in recognition of their guidance and presence. By connecting with the elemental forces, practitioners can harmonize with the natural world and tune into the cosmic rhythms.

After creating the sacred space, the practitioners can move on to the central part of the ritual, which could involve chanting, singing, dancing, meditation, prayer, or spellwork, among other things. These exercises are frequently intended to concentrate the energy and intention of the practitioners, enabling them to strengthen their relationship with the divine and, more powerfully, materialize their wishes. Another possible aspect of rituals is inviting specific deities, spirits, or energies to support the job.

Following the ritual, practitioners can offer gratitude and offerings to the elements and the land itself, as well as to any deities, spirits, or energies called upon throughout the ceremony. This could be making drinks, presenting food or other presents, or just saying "thank you" in a prayer or meditation. After the ritual, the circle can be opened to release the rising energies and let them return to their original state.

Athames, or ritual knives, candles, incense, chalices, pentacles, crystals, and other objects having symbolic or personal meaning may also be used by practitioners during the ceremony. By using these tools, practitioners can concentrate their energies, intensify their goals, and establish a physical link with the heavenly powers they are calling out. By including these instruments in their rituals, practitioners can improve their spiritual practice and strengthen their connection to the universe's profound mysteries.

In summary, a Wiccan ritual is intended to establish a holy space where practitioners can honor the cycles of nature, establish a connection with the divine, and use energy work and focused intention to actualize their wishes. Practitioners can establish a robust container for spiritual development, change, and healing by adhering to a disciplined procedure that incorporates the casting of a circle, the calling forth of elemental forces, and the use of instruments and symbols. Practitioners can co-create a reality in harmony with their highest good, strengthen their connection to the divine, and align themselves with cosmic rhythms via consistent practice and purpose.

Casting the Circle

A key component of Wiccan spirituality is casting the circle, which establishes holy space, calls forth divine forces, and supports ceremonial ceremonies and magical activities. The circle serves as a protection barrier, keeping the sacred area inside from the outer world and forming a space where spiritual activity can be done securely and efficiently.

The practitioner or practitioners usually draw the circle's outline on the ground first, using objects like stones, candles, or wands to delineate the circle's boundaries. This physical barrier is a concrete image of the energetic barrier forming between the outside world and the inner sacred area. The practitioners can see a sphere of protecting energy encircling them while they draw the circle, enclosing the holy area and keeping it closed from outside influences.

The practitioners can then invoke the powers of the five elements—Spirit, Air, Fire, Water, and Earth—to bless and sanctify the area after the circle has been physically drawn out. This can entail asking for the blessings of the elements, contacting their spirits or guardians, and making prayers or invocations in recognition of their guidance and presence. By connecting with the elemental forces, practitioners can harmonize with the natural world and tune into the cosmic rhythms.

Practitioners may also picture a sphere of white or golden light forming about them as the circle is cast and the elemental forces are called upon. This visualization strengthens the protective barrier and establishes a sacred area brimming with blessings and divine energy. By using this visualization, the practitioners' connection to the divine forces they are calling forth is strengthened, and the circle's potency is enhanced.

The practitioners can begin the major part of the ritual or magical work when the circle has been cast and the sacred area prepared. Activities that take place inside the circle and are charged with the energy and intention raised during the circle's casting include meditation, prayer, chanting, singing, dancing, and spellwork.

Upon completion of the ritual or magical activity, the practitioners may offer gratitude and offerings to the elements, the land itself, and the deities, spirits, or energies called upon throughout the ritual. This could be making drinks, presenting food or other presents, or just saying "thank you" in a prayer or meditation. After the ritual, the circle can be opened to release the rising energies and let them return to their original state.

In conclusion, casting the circle is a potent and transforming spiritual activity used in Wicca that helps to create holy space, call forth divine forces, and promote spiritual development. By drawing the circle's boundaries, calling upon the energies of the elements, and envisioning a shield of energy encircling them, practitioners establish a robust framework for magical work and ceremonial rites. Practitioners can co-create a reality in harmony with their highest good, strengthen their connection to the divine, and align themselves with cosmic rhythms via consistent practice and purpose.

Invoking the Elements and Deities

Invoking the elements and deities is a holy rite essential to Wiccan spirituality rituals, ceremonies, and magical operations. Practitioners aim to harmonize with natural forces, establish a connection with the divine, and utilize the powers of creation to bring their goals and wishes to life by calling upon the energies of Earth, Air, Fire, Water, and Spirit, along with particular deities or spirits.

The practitioner usually faces the cardinal directions—north, east, south, and west—and invokes the forces connected to each one to begin the elemental invocation. To bless and sanctify the area, the practitioner may call upon the energy of Earth in the north, utilizing its attributes of stability, grounding, and plenty. To bring inspiration and insight into the ritual, the practitioner may call upon the energy of Air in the east, utilizing its attributes of intellect, communication, and clarity. To kindle the flames of spiritual growth and manifestation, the practitioner may call upon the energy of Fire in the south by invoking its attributes of passion, transformation, and action. To cleanse and purify the area, the practitioner in the west may call upon the energy of Water and its attributes of emotion, intuition, and healing.

Practitioners may call upon specific deities or spirits to assist in their magical operations and rituals and call upon the energies of the elements. By calling upon the presence and blessings of these deities, practitioners hope to strengthen their relationship with the divine, receive direction and inspiration, and develop a sense of reverence and awe for the universe's sacred mysteries. These deities can come from various pantheons and traditions or be ancestors or personal spirits with special meanings for the practitioner.

Prayers, invocations, or chants expressing the practitioner's intentions and goals, along with their awe and appreciation for the energies being invoked, are usually performed in tandem with the invocation of the elements and deities. Depending on the practitioner's tastes and customs, these prayers can be repeated silently or aloud. In addition, gifts such as food or drink may be offered in addition to them as a sign of respect and courtesy to the entities being called upon.

After calling upon the elements and deities and blessing and sanctifying the holy place, practitioners can move on to the main body of the ritual or magical work. Invoking the elements and deities to create a sacred container allows for performing various rituals and practices, including meditation, spellwork, chanting, singing, dancing, and divination.

Upon completion of the magical work or ritual, practitioners can offer gratitude and offerings to the deities and elements and any other spirits or energies called upon during the ritual. This could be making drinks, presenting food or other presents, or just saying "thank you" in a prayer or meditation. After the ritual, the circle can be opened to release the rising energies and let them return to their original state.

To sum up, calling upon the elements and deities is a revered ritual in Wicca that helps practitioners strengthen their magical operations and rites while also bringing them into harmony with the natural world and the supernatural. Practitioners aim to materialize their desires, enhance their spiritual consciousness, and foster a stronger bond with the universe's precious secrets by utilizing elemental forces and particular deities or spirits. Practitioners can co-create a world that aligns with their highest good and strengthen their relationship with the elements and deities via consistent practice and purpose.

CHAPTER VIII

Spellcraft and Magick

Ethics of Spellcasting

Spellcraft and magick are powerful tools used in Wiccan spirituality for manifestation, healing, and spiritual growth. However, with great power comes great responsibility, and Wiccan practitioners are often guided by a set of ethics and principles when casting spells. These ethics serve as a moral compass, guiding practitioners to use their magick in ways that are ethical, responsible, and aligned with their highest good and the greater good of all beings.

The Wiccan Rede, which reads, "An' it harm none, do what ye will," is one of the fundamental moral precepts of Wicca and spellcasting. The significance of weighing the possible outcomes of one's acts and making sure they don't damage or violate the free will of others is emphasized by this principle.

Another ethical consideration in spellcraft is the concept of consent. Practitioners are encouraged to obtain consent from all parties before casting spells that may affect them directly. This includes obtaining consent from others before casting spells on their behalf and obtaining consent from the spirits, deities, or energies being invoked in the spell. By respecting the autonomy and free will of others, practitioners can ensure that their magick is conducted in an ethical and respectful way.

Furthermore, practitioners are encouraged to take responsibility for the consequences of their magickal actions. This means being mindful of the intentions behind their spells and their potential impact on themselves and others. Practitioners are encouraged to know their motivations, ensuring their spells align with their highest intentions and values. Additionally, students are urged to be ready to accept the results of their spells, whether or not they turn out as planned, and to take responsibility for any unforeseen consequences that could occur.

In addition to the Wiccan Rede, practitioners may also adhere to other ethical guidelines and principles regarding spellcasting. These may include principles such as compassion, integrity, and humility, which guide practitioners to use their magick to promote healing, empowerment, and spiritual growth for themselves and others. By aligning their magickal practice with these ethical principles, practitioners can ensure that their spells are conducted with integrity and intention and contribute to the greater good of all beings.

It is also essential for practitioners to be mindful of magick's potential misuse or abuse. While magic can be a powerful tool for transformation and healing, it can also be misused for selfish or harmful purposes. Practitioners are encouraged to use their magick responsibly and to refrain from casting spells that seek to manipulate or control others, infringe upon their free will, or cause harm in any way. By exercising discernment and integrity in their magickal practice, practitioners can ensure that their spells are conducted in a way that is ethical, responsible, and aligned with their highest values and intentions.

In conclusion, Wicca's spellcasting ethics are based on principles of responsibility, respect, and integrity. Practitioners are guided by the Wiccan Rede and other ethical principles to use their magick in ways that promote healing, harmony, and positive transformation while also respecting the free will and autonomy of others. By aligning their magickal practice with these ethical principles, practitioners can ensure that their spells are conducted with integrity, intention, and mindfulness and contribute to the greater good of all beings. Through ethical spellcraft, practitioners can harness the transformative power of magick to create positive change in their lives and the world around them.

Crafting Effective Spells

A key component of Wiccan spirituality is the creation of potent spells, which enable practitioners to use energy, symbolism, and intention to manifest their goals and aspirations. Although casting spells can be an extraordinarily individualized and intuitive process, there are some guidelines and methods practitioners can follow to assist them in designing robust, targeted, and aligned with their highest good.

Clarity of aim is one of the most critical aspects of creating powerful spells. It is advised that practitioners clearly state their objectives and desires—particularly about what they hope to produce or accomplish—before casting a spell. This clarity guarantees that the spell's energy is focused on a specific objective or result and helps to focus it. It might benefit practitioners to put their intentions down in a concise and understandable statement they can refer to when casting spells.

Spellcrafting relies heavily on symbolism in addition to purpose clarity. Symbols are effective means of reaching the subconscious and accessing the most profound levels of awareness. Practitioners can use candles, crystals, colors, and sigils in their spells by incorporating symbols that align with their aims and objectives. Through powerful and significant symbols, practitioners can enhance the power of their spells and establish a closer bond with the forces of creation.

Elevating and directing energy is a crucial part of creating powerful spells. Spells are powered by energy, which practitioners must learn to harness and channel to get the desired results properly. Practitioners can increase and focus their energy by using techniques like breathing, drumming, chanting, dancing, and visualizing to give their spells more strength and intention. Practitioners can increase the strength and efficacy of their spells by developing a strong and focused energy flow.

In spell crafting, timing is another crucial factor. Spellcasters may decide to perform spells in conjunction with astrological events, planetary alignments, or particular phases of the moon. For example, different moon phases are linked to distinct energies and intents; for instance, spells aimed at expansion and manifestation work best with a waxing moon, while spells aimed at banishing and releasing work best with a declining moon. Practitioners may increase the power and efficiency of their spells by arranging them to correspond with the universe's natural rhythms and cycles.

Practitioners may add correspondences like colors, herbs, and crystals to better match their spells with their aims. To increase the efficacy of their spells, practitioners might choose herbs, crystals, and colors that resonate with their aims and desires. Each has its energy and symbolism. Rose quartz, for instance, can be used in spells for compassion and love, while amethyst can be used in spells for intuition and spiritual development.

To sum up, creating potent spells is both an art and a science that calls for time, correspondence, symbolism, energy work, and goal clarity. Spells can be concentrated, potent, and aligned with the highest benefit of the practitioner by articulating intentions clearly, choosing powerful symbols, raising and directing energy, connecting with the natural rhythms and cycles of the universe, and incorporating correspondences. Magick practitioners can refine their spell-crafting abilities and harness the transformational force of magick to manifest their intents and desires for their highest good via consistent practice and intention.

Common Spells and Their Purposes

In Wiccan spirituality, spells are powerful tools for manifesting intentions, healing, protection, and spiritual growth. While the possibilities for spellwork are virtually limitless, several common types of spells are frequently used by practitioners for various purposes.

One common type is the love spell, used to attract love, enhance romantic relationships, or bring about reconciliation between partners. Love spells may involve using herbs, crystals, candles, and other correspondences associated with love and romance, as well as visualization and intention-setting techniques to focus the spell's energy. These spells can improve a relationship, draw in a particular love partner, or mend emotional scars associated with relationships and love.

Another common type of spell is the prosperity spell, which is used to attract abundance, wealth, and financial success. Prosperity spells may involve using herbs, crystals, candles, and other correspondences associated with prosperity and abundance, as well as visualization and affirmation techniques to focus the spell's energy. These spells may manifest a specific financial goal, attract new opportunities for success, or remove blocks and obstacles that may hinder abundance.

Protection spells are also commonly used in Wiccan spirituality to ward off negative energies, psychic attacks, and harmful influences. These spells may involve using herbs, crystals, candles, and other correspondences associated with protection and warding, as well as visualization and energy shielding techniques to generate a protective barrier around oneself or one's home. Protection spells may be performed regularly as a preventative measure, or in response to specific threats or challenges that may arise.

Healing spells are another common type used in Wiccan spirituality to promote physical, emotional, and spiritual well-being. These spells may involve herbs, crystals, candles, and other correspondences associated with healing and wellness, as well as visualization, energy healing, and prayer techniques to facilitate healing. Healing spells may alleviate physical ailments, heal emotional wounds, or restore balance and harmony to the body, mind, and spirit.

In addition to these common types of spells, practitioners may also perform spells for various other purposes, such as spiritual growth, empowerment, divination, and protection of the environment. These spells may involve a wide range of techniques and correspondences, depending on the spell's specific intention and desired outcome. For example, spells for spiritual growth may include meditation, visualization, and energy work techniques to deepen one's connection with the divine and expand one's consciousness.

Spells can be an effective tool for bringing about positive change and achieving goals, but it's crucial to remember that they should always be used carefully and with ethical judgment. Practitioners should weigh the possible outcomes of their spells and make sure they serve both their own highest benefit and the greater welfare of all creatures. Magick practitioners can use the transformational power of magick to make positive changes in their lives and the world around them by approaching spellwork with mindfulness, intention, and integrity.

CHAPTER IX

Deities and Divine Connection

Pantheons and Wiccan Deities

A fundamental aspect of Wiccan spirituality is the concept of divinity, which informs practitioners' religious and magical practices. Deities are believed to embody divine energy representing various facets of the universe, the natural world, and the human experience. Although Wicca is a decentralized religion without a central body or set of beliefs, its adherents frequently take their magical practices and acts of worship from other myths and pantheons.

Wiccan spirituality is notable for its polytheistic nature, which recognizes the existence of numerous deities and divine entities. Wiccans may worship and interact with gods from many cultural and religious traditions, such as the Greek, Roman, Egyptian, Celtic, Norse, and Hindu pantheons. Every tradition has its own pantheon of gods and goddesses, each with its own qualities, legends, and emblems.

In Wiccan mysticism, one of the most frequently summoned deities are the Horned God and the Triple Goddess, who stand for divinity's feminine and male facets. The Triple Goddess is regarded as the phases of the moon, the cycles of life, from maiden to mother to crone, while the Horned God is frequently connected to the wildness of nature, the hunt, and the cycle of life, death, and rebirth. The Triple Goddess and the Horned God constitute a divine alliance for the cosmos' harmony and balance of feminine and masculine energy.

Depending on their spiritual path and tastes, Wiccans may engage with a wide range of additional deities and supernatural beings in addition to the Horned God and the Triple Goddess. While some practitioners may deal with a wide range of deities from many traditions, others may concentrate their worship and magical operations on specific deities from a particular pantheon. The objective is always the same, regardless of the specific deities invoked: strengthening one's bond with the divine and developing a respectful, loving, and trusting relationship with the gods and goddesses.

Invoking the presence and benefits of elemental entities like faeries, sprites, and nature spirits can also be a part of Wiccan rituals and magical practices. Practitioners can engage with these entities to seek direction, protection, and healing because they are believed to be guardians and protectors of the natural environment. Practitioners want to have a closer relationship with nature and live in balance with its powers by honoring and respecting the elemental beings.

Ultimately, Wiccan spirituality's deity worship and working practice are very subjective and individualized. It leaves practitioners free to select the gods and supernatural entities most closely aligned with their experiences, values, and beliefs. The objective is always the same, regardless of whether one is calling upon the ancient gods and goddesses of a specific pantheon or engaging with an ancestor or personal spirits: to strengthen one's bond with the divine and to foster an atmosphere of respect, love, and confidence with the gods and goddesses. Those practicing aim to harmonize with the divine will and co-create a world that serves both their highest benefit and the greater welfare of all beings through worship, devotion, and magic.

Building Relationships with Deities

For many practitioners of Wicca and other pagan traditions, developing connections with deities is a fundamental part of their spiritual practice. These connections—founded on reverence, respect, and devotion—give practitioners the chance to strengthen their bond with the divine and receive direction, encouragement, and inspiration for their spiritual journey.

The practice of daily devotion and worship is one of the foundational ideas in developing a relationship with deities. A practitioner's daily or weekly schedule can include rituals, prayers, offerings, and meditation to honor and worship the deities of their choice. These customs include offering food or drink, lighting candles, making incense, and saying prayers or invocations to call upon the gods and goddesses for protection and blessings. Those who do devotional practices want a closer relationship with the gods and goddesses and a sense of closeness and intimacy with the divine.

Practitioners may establish personal connections and communication with deities in addition to their ordinary worship. This could include praying, meditating, or using divination methods to ask the gods and goddesses for wisdom, insight, and inspiration. To pay respect and gratitude to their chosen deities for their favors, practitioners can also do deeds of service or devotion. Through active interaction with the gods and goddesses, practitioners aim to create a meaningful and intimate relationship with the supernatural founded on mutual love, respect, and trust.

Studying the gods' myths, symbols, and characteristics is a crucial part of developing a relationship with them. Scholarly publications, mythology books, and sacred texts can all be read by practitioners to get additional knowledge about the traits, narratives, and attributes of the gods they have selected. To gain a deeper grasp of each deity's energies and effects, they may also study the correspondences linked to them, which include things like colors, gemstones, and medicines. Through immersing oneself in the mythology and lore of the gods and goddesses, practitioners want to strengthen their connection to their essence and presence and gain a more profound respect and admiration for their divine attributes.

Additionally, practitioners may establish relationships with deities by performing deeds of devotion and service. In addition to participating in rites, celebrations, and ceremonies that celebrate the gods and goddesses' presence and blessings may entail doing deeds of kindness, generosity, and compassion in their names. Through active acts of service and devotion, practitioners aim to strengthen their connection to the divine energies and influences of the gods and goddesses and express their thanks and reverence for them.

Ultimately, developing a relationship with a deity is a highly subjective and personal process that differs from person to person. There is no one-size-fits-all method to establish relationships with deities, and practitioners are advised to base their spiritual practices on their inspiration, intuition, and guidance. The objective is always the same, whether attained by regular worship, one-on-one interactions, study, or acts of devotion and service: to strengthen one's bond with the divine and develop a respectful, loving, and trustworthy relationship with the gods and goddesses. Through these connections, practitioners hope to connect with the will and purpose of God and receive inspiration, support, and guidance for their spiritual journey.

Devotional Practices

Many spiritual traditions, including Wicca and other pagan paths, are based on holy rituals. These rituals, which entail acts of respect, adoration, and devotion to the divine, are essential to strengthening practitioners' ties to the sacred and helping them develop a sense of purpose and spiritual fulfillment.

Ritual worship is one of the most popular devotional practices among Wiccans. To do this, you might have to dedicate a specific period each day or week to rituals that respect and worship the gods and goddesses and other spiritual creatures like ancestors and nature spirits. Offerings of food, drink, or other presents, prayers, invocations, and meditation practices to call upon the divine's blessings and presence are some examples of these rituals. Ritual worshippers aim to establish a sacred environment to communicate with the gods and goddesses, get inspiration and guidance, and strengthen their bond with the divine.

The observance of sacred festivals and holidays, known as Sabbats and Esbats, is another significant devotional activity in Wicca. Observing the seasonal and lunar cycles, these celebrations offer practitioners a chance to commemorate the universe's great secrets and pay homage to the gods and goddesses via ritual, food, and camaraderie. Wiccan spirituality specializes in sabbats like Samhain, Beltane, and Lammas because they symbolize significant moments in the cosmic and agricultural cycles and offer personal development opportunities.

In Wicca, prayer is another popular devotional activity that enables practitioners to speak with the gods and goddesses directly and to convey their wishes, appreciation, and respect. Prayers can be silent or uttered out loud, and they can take on many forms, ranging from straightforward requests for protection, healing, or direction to sincere expressions of gratitude and blessings. Through consistent prayer, believers aim to develop a close relationship and understanding with God and to be in harmony with the divine plan and intention.

Another significant devotional technique in Wicca is meditation, which enables practitioners to open their hearts, calm their brains, and connect with the divine presence both within and outside oneself. As part of ritual worship or spiritual gatherings, meditation can be done independently or in groups using techniques like mindfulness, visualization, or breathwork. Using meditation, practitioners aim to enhance their relationship with the divine and become more attuned to the patterns and forces of the universe.

In Wicca, service and kindness are significant religious activities that enable practitioners to show their love and respect for the divine by being nice to others and serving them. Practitioners can participate in community-building events and rituals that support healing, harmony, and well-being, as well as charitable, volunteer, and environmental stewardship deeds in the name of the gods and goddesses. Practitioners aim to live out the core principles of Wiccan spirituality—love, compassion, and generosity—by serving others and serving as vehicles for the divine will.

To sum up, devotion to the gods and goddesses is essential to Wiccan spirituality. It allows practitioners to revere and adore the deities, strengthen their relationship with the divine, and develop a sense of purpose and spiritual fulfillment. Devotional activities, whether acts of kindness, prayer, meditation, ceremonial worship, or service, enable practitioners to show their love and regard for the sacred and connect themselves with God's will and purpose. By consistently engaging in these activities, practitioners want to embody the core ideals of Wiccan spirituality—love, compassion, and harmony—and to strengthen their relationship with the divine.

CHAPTER X

Nature and Animism

Sacredness of Nature

The Wiccan faith sees Nature as sacred and endowed with divine force. The belief in animism, which holds that all living things, including the Earth itself, have a spiritual essence or soul, is the source of this respect for the natural world. Animism holds that all living things, including rocks, trees, plants, and animals, are manifestations of the divine and that the natural world is alive with consciousness, intelligence, and life. Wicca's philosophy is based on the understanding that Nature is sacred, which shapes many of its activities and beliefs.

The idea that everything is interrelated is one of the main pillars of Wiccan spirituality. Practitioners see themselves as entwined with Nature's elements, plants, animals, and spirits and as part of a more excellent web of life. In rituals, rites, and everyday life, this interconnectivity is recognized and honored as a mirror of the divine unity that underpins all existence. Practitioners aim to develop a stronger sense of harmony and connection with the Earth and its inhabitants by acknowledging and respecting the holiness of Nature.

In Wiccan spirituality, the natural environment is also seen as an origin of wisdom, healing, and spiritual insight. Practitioners frequently go to Nature for direction, inspiration, and rejuvenation; they find comfort in the majesty and beauty of the natural world. Spending time in Nature, whether through hikes in the forest, meditation by rivers, or just sitting in peaceful contemplation under trees, is found by practitioners to be beneficial for calming the mind, uplifting the soul, and acclimating oneself to the cycles and rhythms of the planet.

Besides its spiritual significance, Nature is a practical source of magical power and energy in the Wiccan faith. Mana, also called chi, is the energy practitioners who believe it exists in the natural world and maybe channeled and harnessed for magical operations and rituals. Practitioners can use this energy, thought to flow through all living things and natural objects, in their rituals and spellwork to bring their intents and aspirations to life. Practitioners aim to align themselves with the natural energies of creation and increase the strength of their magic by working in harmony with the natural world.

The Wiccan regard for the elements—Earth, Air, Fire, Water, and Spirit—also reflects Nature's holiness. These elements, which stand for various facets of the natural and supernatural realms, are said to be the fundamental components of the universe. In their rituals and ceremonies, practitioners revere and call upon the energies of the elements to become attuned to their characteristics and vibrations. Practitioners aim to link themselves with the elemental forces of creation and strengthen their connection to the natural world through working with the elements.

In addition, Wiccan spirituality strongly emphasizes conservation and environmental stewardship as means of respecting and preserving the holiness of the natural world. Practitioners understand the interdependence of all life and the potential effects of human activity on the planet's health and vitality. By reducing their ecological imprint and supporting laws and procedures that advance sustainability and biodiversity, they work to live in balance with the environment. Practitioners want to respect the holiness of Nature, so future generations ions can continue to enjoy its wealth and beauty by taking caring for and its inhabitants.

To sum up, the core of Wiccan spirituality is the sacredness of Nature, which shapes its practices, beliefs, and ideals. Practitioners consider Nature sacred and see it as a wellspring of knowledge, healing, and enlightenment. Through acknowledging the interdependence of all things, valuing the elements, and engaging in ecological responsibility, adherents want to enhance their bond with the natural world and harmonize with the divine powers of creation. Practitioners aim to develop a stronger feeling of connectedness, harmony, and reverence for the Earth and its inhabitants via their reverence for Nature.

Communing with Nature Spirits

The natural world is respected in Wiccan theology and is also believed to be home to many invisible creatures known as nature spirits. These spirits, sometimes called sprites, elementals, or faeries, are said to be the keepers and protectors of the natural world, keeping an eye on the cycles of life and death as well as the harmony and balance of the elements. Through communion with nature spirits, individuals can connect with these elusive entities, pay tribute to their existence, and ask for their wisdom and blessings on their spiritual path.

Ritual and ceremony-based communication with nature spirits is one of the most popular methods. To commemorate and call upon the presence of nature spirits, practitioners may erect altars or shrines in outdoor areas like fields, gardens, or forests. While prayers, invocations, and songs can be spoken to connect and communicate with the spirits, offerings of food, drink, flowers, or other presents can be presented to gain their attention and favor. Practitioners want to create a holy environment where they can communicate with the spirits of nature and receive their blessings and guidance through ritual and ceremony.

Using meditation and visualization techniques is another method to communicate with nature spirits. Sitting peacefully outdoors, practitioners can close their eyes and concentrate on their surroundings' sensations, sounds, and scents. Then, they might see themselves achieving a level of oneness with the nature spirits, inviting them to meditate and have telepathic or impressionistic communication. Practitioners aim to tune into the subtle energies and vibrations of the nature spirits and accept their messages and guidance by stilling the mind and opening the heart.

Another significant way to communicate with nature spirits is through offerings and deeds of service. To show their appreciation and respect for the nature spirits' presence and contributions, practitioners can offer them food, drink, or other items. To respect nature and show their dedication to its preservation, they could also perform deeds of service like gardening, tree planting, or litter cleanup. To make a relationship based on reciprocity and respect with the nature spirits and to express gratitude for the treasures of the Earth, practitioners make offerings and serve others.

Connecting with nature spirits and asking for their wisdom and direction can also be accomplished through divination and oracle methods. Using instruments like pendulums, scrying mirrors, or oracle cards, practitioners can communicate with the spirits and get their advice and messages. Practitioners can connect with the wisdom and understanding of the nature spirits by asking questions or seeking assistance on particular difficulties. In return, they will receive answers and insights to benefit them on their spiritual journey and daily lives.

Additionally, communicating with nature spirits may be a very intuitive and intimate experience. Simply spending time in nature, taking in the wonder and beauty of their surroundings, and allowing themselves to be receptive to the advice and presence of nature spirits can be enough for practitioners. Practitioners aim to develop a profound sense of reverence, gratitude, and connection with the natural spirits and to acknowledge their presence and blessings in their lives, whether via silent contemplation, prayer, meditation, or acts of service.

In conclusion, Wiccan spirituality views communicating with nature spirits as a sacred and profoundly important practice that enables practitioners to connect with the elusive entities living in the natural world and ask for their advice and blessings on their spiritual path. To cultivate a relationship of respect, gratitude, and reciprocity with the nature spirits and to honor their presence and blessings in their lives, practitioners employ ritual and ceremony, meditation and visualization, offerings and acts of service, divination and oracle techniques, as well as personal intuition and connection. By communicating with nature spirits, practitioners want to strengthen their bond with the environment and live in balance with its cycles and rhythms, respecting the holiness of all life and the interdependence of all things.

Eco-Spirituality and Environmentalism

Eco-spirituality is a comprehensive approach to spirituality that highlights the holiness of the natural world and acknowledges the interconnection of all life. This belief system aims to cultivate a profound reverence, gratitude, and responsibility for the world and its people while honoring the Earth as a living, conscious entity. Fundamentally, eco-spirituality recognizes that humans are an essential component of the biosphere and that the health and vitality of the Earth are closely related to each other.

On the other hand, environmentalism is a social and political movement that supports the preservation and conservation of the environment and the sustainable use of the resources found on Earth. In addition to advocating for laws and practices that support ecological balance and environmental sustainability, it aims to address problems including pollution, habitat degradation, species extinction, and climate change. Environmentalism and eco-spirituality are sometimes perceived as two separate movements, although they are closely associated and adhere to many of the same ideals.

The idea that nature is sacred is one of the central tenets of eco-spirituality. Eco-spiritualists acknowledge every living creature's intrinsic worth and dignity and see it as a living, breathing entity brimming with consciousness. They strive to develop a profound reverence and thankfulness for the Earth and its inhabitants because they consider the natural world a manifestation of the divine, full of beauty, wonder, and wisdom. Eco-spiritualists want to create a closer bond with the natural world and live in balance with its cycles and rhythms by respecting the holiness of the natural world.

The conviction that all life is interrelated is a crucial tenet of eco-spirituality. Eco-spiritualists understand that our actions affect the web of life and that a vast and complex web of relationships connects us all. They recognize that the health and vitality of the Earth are directly related to human well-being and that we must safeguard the Earth and its people. Eco-spiritualists strive to promote empathy, compassion, solidarity with the natural world, and the welfare of all living things by recognizing our connectivity with all life.

Many beliefs and ideas of environmentalism and eco-spirituality are similar, such as a strong reverence for the Earth and a dedication to environmental care. The ecological catastrophes our world is experiencing, such as pollution, deforestation, habitat destruction, and climate change, must be addressed immediately.

Environmentalists also advocate for laws and practices to safeguard the environment for future generations. They fight to increase public understanding of the significance of ecological balance and environmental sustainability and support policies like renewable energy, conservation, sustainable agriculture, and wildlife protection.

Environmentalism and eco-spirituality are lived practices that influence how we interact with the natural world and daily decisions. They are not merely theories or abstract beliefs. By decreasing their carbon footprint, conserving energy and water, minimizing waste, supporting locally owned and sustainable companies, and promoting environmental justice and equity, eco-spiritualists and environmentalists want to live out their principles. They understand that even tiny deeds of compassion and generosity toward the environment can have a significant impact, motivating others to act and bringing about good change on a bigger scale.

To sum up, eco-spirituality and environmentalism are closely related belief systems that strongly emphasize the value of environmental stewardship, the holiness of nature, and the interdependence of all life. Eco-spiritualists and environmentalists aim to foster a profound reverence, gratitude, and responsibility for the Earth and all its inhabitants by acknowledging Earth as a living, sentient creature and our interconnectedness with all life. By their attitudes and deeds, they strive to make the world more equitable, sustainable, and peaceful for the next generations.

CHAPTER XI

Divination and Intuition

Methods of Divination (Tarot, Runes, Scrying)

Using supernatural methods to discover hidden truths or the future is known as divination. It is an age-old craft that has been utilized for ages by civilizations worldwide, and it is still a well-liked and extensively utilized resource for spiritual insight and direction. The foundation of divination is the idea that invisible energy and forces, which are accessible and comprehensible via various means, control the cosmos.

The Tarot is among the most well-liked and frequently applied divination techniques. Each card represents various archetypal energies, symbols, and meanings in the Tarot deck used for divination. In a tarot reading, the cards are usually shuffled before a specific number of cards are drawn from the deck and interpreted by the reader to offer direction and understanding to a given query or problem. The Tarot is an adaptable and flexible instrument that may be used for many things, such as relationships and love, work and money, spiritual development, and personal progress.

Using runes is another common divination technique. The Norse and other Germanic peoples employed runes as ancient symbols for writing, sorcery, and divination. Usually composed of clay, stone, or wood, each rune is engraved with a unique meaning and symbol. The standard procedure for rune readings is to draw a certain number of runes from a bag or pouch and analyze their associations and meanings to offer direction and understanding on a specific topic or matter. Runes are frequently utilized to answer issues about decision-making, spiritual insight, and personal development.

Another divination technique practiced for centuries by tribes worldwide is scrying. To practice scrying, one must look into a reflective object, such as a bowl of water, a mirror, or a crystal ball, and let one's mind calm and open. Through this procedure, practitioners may obtain insights and assistance on a specific concern or issue through visions, images, or impressions. Scrying is very subjective and intuitive, depending on the practitioner's interpretation of the symbols and images that appear.

Although every divination method has distinct qualities and methods, they all aim to give the practitioner insight, direction, and clarity on important issues. Rather than making exact predictions, divination aims to comprehend ourselves better and the world around us by drawing on the wisdom and direction of the cosmos. It is a tool for introspection, personal development, and spiritual understanding. It can also be a helpful ally on the path to empowerment and self-discovery.

Tarot, runes, and scrying are valuable tools for developing and refining intuition in addition to being used for divination. The capacity to obtain information and insight without the need for conscious thought or logical analysis is known as intuition, and it is a valuable ability that may be developed with practice. Practitioners can develop their intuition and access wisdom and guidance through scrying, runes, and tarot cards.

Scrying, Tarot, and runes are other valuable tools for developing psychic talents and establishing spiritual connections. Regular practice and meditation can help practitioners become more aware of the subtle energies and forces that shape their lives and strengthen their relationship with the divine. By learning to comprehend the signs and symbols that surface during readings, they can have a deeper comprehension of the messages and directions they receive.

To sum up, scrying, runes, and Tarot are effective instruments for spiritual insight, intuition, and divination. They provide practitioners with a way to understand themselves and the world around them better and access the universe's wisdom and direction. Tarot, Runes, and scrying are valuable tools for self-discovery and empowerment, enabling practitioners to access their inner wisdom and confidently navigate life's opportunities and challenges. These tools can be used for divination, personal growth, and spiritual development.

Developing Intuitive Abilities

Often referred to as an inner knowing or gut instinct, intuition is a strong, natural human ability that gives us access to knowledge and understanding outside the boundaries of reason and logic. Gaining intuitive skills can significantly improve our lives by assisting us in making sensible decisions, offering clarity when things are unclear, and enabling us to handle life's challenges more efficiently and confidently. Even though some people might be born with excellent intuitive skills, intuition is a skill that can be improved and refined with effort, perseverance, and self-awareness.

Developing self-awareness and mindfulness skills is one of the best methods to become more intuitive. Regular meditation can help practitioners learn to calm their minds, focus on the here and now, and become more perceptive of the subtle messages and feelings inside them. By practicing mindfulness meditation, individuals can become more conscious of their thoughts, emotions, and physical sensations, which will help them distinguish between outside influences and their inner direction. Through mindfulness of their inner mind and body, practitioners can identify the intuitive cues and insights that present themselves naturally. They can then learn to trust and confidently act upon these insights.

Learning to believe in and heed one's instincts is crucial to becoming intuitive. Our intuition communicates subtly through sensations, instincts, and gut reactions that don't always make sense. Developing intuitive abilities requires learning to trust these intuitive promptings and follow through on them, even when they appear illogical or nonsensical. By paying attention to and obeying our inner direction, we can start to build stronger intuitive muscles and develop a stronger sense of trust and confidence in our own intuition.

Another valuable technique for honing intuition is listening actively to synchronicities and signals from the cosmos. Symbols, signs, and synchronicities—such as repeating numbers, significant coincidences, or chance meetings—are common ways intuition speaks to us. Practitioners can learn to interpret and comprehend the information supplied to them and use it to guide their decisions and actions by remaining open and receptive to these indications and messages. We can prosper in a powerful relationship with our intuition and the universe's wisdom by deliberately searching out and observing the signs and synchronicities in our lives.

Cultivating openness, curiosity, and receptivity to the unknown is another essential part of developing intuitive talents. When accessing more profound levels of wisdom and insight that are not easily accessible to the rational mind, intuition frequently functions outside the boundaries of conscious consciousness. Through accepting ambiguity and letting go of control, practitioners can make room for intuition to grow and develop organically. By adopting an open and curious outlook on life, practitioners can create a stronger bond with their intuitive selves and the secrets of the cosmos.

Developing intuitive skills can also be aided by engaging in imaginative activities and artistic expression. Since creativity and intuition are closely related, pursuing creative endeavors like writing, music, dancing, or art can aid in revealing our innate capacity for intuition. By embracing the creative process and letting ideas come to them without inhibition or judgment, practitioners can reach new levels of intuition and insight and improve their clarity and comprehension of the outside world and themselves.

To sum up, cultivating intuitive skills is a path of self-awareness and empowerment that can significantly improve our lives and overall well-being. We can access the wisdom that resides within us and always available guidance and insight by developing mindfulness and self-awareness, learning to trust and follow our instincts, embracing uncertainty, paying attention to signs and synchronicities, and creating art. We may learn to have a stronger relationship with our intuition and become more adept at navigating the intricacies of life with elegance, clarity, and confidence by practicing, being patient, and being self-aware.

Using Divination in Daily Practice

For ages, nations worldwide have employed divination—using supernatural methods to gain insight and guidance—as a tool for decision-making, personal growth, and spiritual advancement. Although divination has historically been connected to fortune-telling and future prediction, it may also help obtain insight, knowledge, and direction in our day-to-day activities. By integrating divination into our routine, we can draw on the expertise and direction of the cosmos to help us overcome obstacles in life, make wise choices, and develop a closer relationship with the outside world and ourselves.

Using oracle cards in divination is one of the most popular methods used in everyday practice. Oracle cards are decks of cards with distinct images, symbols, or messages on each card used for divination. In an oracle card reading, the cards are usually shuffled before a specific number of cards are drawn from the deck and interpreted to offer advice and insight on a given topic or problem. Oracle cards can be used for various things, such as daily guidance, affirmation, inspiration, and reflection. They are a readily available and multipurpose tool.

Daily tarot or rune draws are another common way divination is used daily. Both runes and tarot are age-old divination methods that can offer insightful advice and direction daily. Drawing one card or rune from the deck daily and considering its meaning and importance is known as a daily tarot or rune draw. This regular practice can offer direction for the day ahead and an understanding of the energy and influences at work in our lives. We can obtain perspective and clarity on the opportunities and challenges ahead by integrating a daily tarot or rune draw into our routine. This allows us to make well-informed decisions that serve our highest good.

In our everyday practice, divination can also be utilized as a tool for goal-setting and intention-setting. Before doing a divination reading, we may focus our energy and attention on a particular aspect of our lives and obtain insight into how to best achieve our goals by asking a specific question or making a clear intention. For instance, we could consult the runes or cards to get advice on overcoming challenges, aligning with our best purpose, or materializing our wishes. We can obtain clarity and concentrate on what we want to create and manifest in our lives by employing divination as a tool for goal-setting. Then, we can take inspired action to make it happen.

Divination can be a tool for self-reflection, personal development, and offering direction and insight. Regular divination readings help us discover subconscious patterns and beliefs that may affect our lives and provide insight into our thoughts, feelings, and behaviors. Divination can enable us to identify areas where we may be trapped or stagnant and provide advice on moving forward with better clarity and purpose. By utilizing divination for introspection and personal development, we can better understand ourselves and our lives and make constructive adjustments that align with our highest good.

Lastly, divination can be a method for developing a closer relationship with the divine and the cosmos' invisible powers. We can strengthen our relationship with our intuition and inner guidance and become more responsive to the wisdom and guidance of the universe by routinely partaking in divination readings. By using divination, we can access the underlying mysteries of existence and gain an understanding of the subtle energies and vibrations surrounding us. By employing divination as a tool for connecting with the divine, we can create a more profound feeling of confidence, faith, and surrender in the unfolding of our lives and align ourselves with the greater purpose and wisdom of the cosmos.

To sum up, divination is an effective and adaptable instrument that we can utilize regularly to obtain understanding, direction, and clarity in our lives. Incorporating divination into our daily routine allows us to reflect on our thoughts and behaviors, create intentions and objectives, negotiate life's problems, and strengthen our connection to the divine. Divination—whether via oracle cards, daily tarot or rune draws, or other methods— can be a helpful ally in self-discovery, personal development, and spiritual awakening.

CHAPTER XII

Astral Travel and Dreamwork

Techniques for Astral Projection

The deliberate departure of the physical body to explore the astral plane, a region of awareness beyond the physical world, is called astral travel, sometimes referred to as astral projection. In contrast, dreamwork is delving into the dream world and gaining access to the subconscious mind to understand, heal, and advance spiritually. Both of these techniques can effectively gain access to higher realms of consciousness, develop spiritual awareness, and expand consciousness. They also present worthwhile chances for introspection, self-discovery, and personal growth.

Relaxation and visualization techniques are one of the most popular methods for astral projection. Usually, practitioners start by practicing gradual muscle relaxation, deep breathing, or meditation to calm the body and mind. Practitioners see themselves flying above their bodies and journeying to various astral realms or dimensions once they have reached peace. Practitioners can achieve heightened awareness and consciousness that enables them to explore the astral plane more clearly and transparently by focusing their attention and intention on the intended destination.

Using brainwave entrainment or binaural beats is another method of astral projection. As part of a sound therapy technique called binaural beats, two slightly different frequencies are listened to in each ear, creating a third frequency representing a particular neural state. Astral projection can be facilitated, and one's ability to access the astral plane is enhanced by listening to binaural beats intended to produce deep relaxation or altered consciousness. Binaural beats can be utilized with relaxation and visualization techniques to improve the heavenly experience and raise the chances of success.

Another effective method for dreamwork and astral projection is meditation. Regular meditation can help practitioners become more conscious of and in control of their thoughts, feelings, and energy. This can improve the clarity and richness of their dream experiences and aid in the process of astral projection. By learning to calm the mind, achieve heightened awareness, and reach more profound levels of consciousness through meditation, practitioners can explore the astral and dream realms more easily.

Lucid dreaming is one of the most potent methods for astral projection. The practice of realizing while in a dream that you are dreaming and having conscious control over and manipulation of the dream world is known as lucid dreaming. Practitioners can achieve transparency and use their dreams as a portal to the astral plane by learning to identify the telltale symptoms of dreaming and developing increased awareness and control over their dreams. Practitioners of lucid dreaming can engage with the dream environment in ways that are not feasible in the real world and explore the astral plane with greater freedom and flexibility.

Lastly, dream journals can be helpful for dreamwork and astral projection. Regular dream journaling allows practitioners to track their progress in astral projection and dream exploration and acquire a more profound understanding of their subconscious mind through identifying recurrent themes and symbols. Keep a dream notebook to gain valuable insights and reflections on your inner journey. It can also be a source of inspiration and guidance for future astral travel and dreamwork experiences.

Dreamwork and astral travel are effective methods for introspection, self-awareness, and metamorphosis. Through lucid dreaming, binaural beats, relaxation techniques, journaling, meditation, and lucid dream training, practitioners can reach higher states of consciousness, spiritual awareness, and a deeper understanding of themselves and their world. Applied singly or in combination, these methods provide priceless chances for discovery, learning, and personal development. They can also effectively raise awareness and solve enigmas related to the dream and astral domains.

Understanding and Interpreting Dreams

Since ancient times, dreams have captivated and enthralled people because they provide a glimpse into the subconscious and reveal our innermost wants, anxieties, and feelings. Even though dreams might initially seem disorganized and absurd, they frequently have hidden meanings and symbols that can offer insightful direction and understanding for the conscious world. Dream interpretation and understanding are skills that can be acquired and cultivated, opening doors to the vast and intricate world of the unconscious and helping us understand the workings of the mind.

Realizing that dreams are highly symbolic is one of the fundamental concepts of dream interpretation and analysis. Symbols are the unconscious mind's language, frequently appearing in dreams as metaphors or illustrations of more profound psychological discoveries and realities. For instance, seeing water in a dream may represent feelings and the subconscious, whereas seeing airplanes in a dream might represent freedom, release, or the wish to escape constraints. We can discover hidden patterns and meanings and gain deeper insight into our innermost thoughts, feelings, and ambitions by learning to identify and understand the symbols that emerge in our dreams.

Realizing how emotions influence dream content is crucial to comprehending and interpreting dreams. Strong psychological forces and emotions frequently significantly influence the themes and tenor of our dreams. On the other hand, dreams that contain joy, excitement, or love may represent feelings of happiness, satisfaction, or contentment in the real world. For instance, dreams filled with fear, worry, or despair may represent unresolved emotional issues or unconscious concerns and anxieties. We can learn more about our emotional states and pinpoint areas where we need to direct our attention and energy to heal and progress by observing the feelings accompanying our dreams.

It's crucial to understand that dreams are incredibly subjective and individualized experiences, and each person's dream will have a different meaning based on their particular situation. The interpretation of a dream ultimately depends on the environment in which it occurs and the connections the dreamer brings to it, even if some symbols may have universal meanings widely recognized throughout cultures and periods. For instance, depending on one's particular experiences and relationships with snakes, dreaming of a snake may represent transformation or rejuvenation for one person while symbolizing fear or danger for another.

Keeping a dream journal is one method for deciphering and interpreting dreams. Dream journals are valuable tools for dream analysis and recording. They let the dreamer monitor reoccurring themes and symbols, spot linkages and patterns, and acquire an understanding of the deeper meanings and messages their dreams might be conveying. By routinely recording their dreams and reflecting on their meaning, dreamers can learn more about their unconscious minds and the problems that might impact their waking lives.

Understanding and interpreting dreams can also be aided by dreamwork techniques like active imagination, dream analysis, and dream interpretation. To understand dreams' underlying meaning and significance, active imagination interacts with their imagery and symbolism through innovative expression, such as writing, painting, or drawing. Dream analysis is dissecting a dream into its parts and looking at how they relate to each other to find hidden themes and patterns. Dream interpretation is deciphering a dream's symbols and visuals to determine their more profound significance and application to the dreamer's life.

In summary, dream interpretation and understanding a skills that can be acquired and practiced, opening doors to the vast and intricate world of the unconscious mind and providing insight into our deepest wants, feelings, and ideas. By applying dreamwork techniques, dream journaling, emotional awareness, and dream recognition, we can obtain insight into the psyche's workings and solve many psychological puzzles. Dreams provide us with a glimpse into the most hidden corners of our brains, and through investigating and analyzing them, we can learn more about the world and ourselves.

Lucid Dreaming Practices

The remarkable phenomenon known as "lucid dreaming" occurs when a person is dreaming and realizes they are dreaming. With this knowledge, a universe of opportunities becomes accessible, enabling the dreamer to shape and control the dreamscape actively, communicate with dream figures, and delve into the recesses of their psyche. The term "lucid dreaming" refers to a range of methods and strategies people can use to develop the capacity to become lucid in their dreams and use the dream realm for spiritual study, creative expression, and personal development.

The development of dream awareness is one of the most essential lucid dreaming techniques. To become aware of one's dreams while still in the dream state is to practice dream awareness. Regular reality checks, which entail easy tests or observations to ascertain if one is awake or dreaming, can help achieve this. Observing the hands, attempting to float or fly, or forcing a finger into the palm of the other hand are standard reality checks. People can teach themselves to become more conscious of their dream state and raise their chances of having lucid dreams by adding reality checks into their everyday routines.

A crucial technique for achieving lucid dreams is making plans before bed. Declaring oneself that one will become lucid in dreams and focusing one's attention on this objective constitutes setting intentions. One way to do this is through visualization, meditation, or even repeating an affirmation or mantra, like "I will become lucid in my dreams tonight." People can boost their chances of having lucid dreams by programming their subconscious mind to be more sensitive to clarity by setting clear and concentrated intentions before going to sleep.

Intention setting and dream awareness are combined in a technique known as mnemonic induction of lucid dreams (MILD) to increase the likelihood of having lucid dreams. After a sleep period, usually in the early morning, people who use the MILD technique wake up and concentrate on their purpose to become lucid in their dreams. They could imagine themselves becoming lucid in a dream, repeat an affirmation or mantra connected to lucid dreaming, and then go back to sleep to become lucid. People can teach themselves to become more aware of their dream state and raise their chances of having lucid dreams by consistently using the MILD technique.

Wake-induced lucid dreaming (WILD) is an additional helpful method for lucid dreaming. By retaining awareness during the shift from waking to sleep, WILD enables a person to go straight into a lucid dream state without losing consciousness. To engage in WILD, practitioners usually lie comfortably and allow themselves to fall asleep while focusing on their breath or a pictured image. They stay conscious and keep their attention on their goal to become coherent even as they start to experience auditory and visual hallucinations, which are the hallmarks of the hypnagogic state. People can consciously enter a lucid dream state and learn to transition from wakefulness to sleep with practice smoothly.

Beyond these techniques, maintaining a dream journal can be an invaluable resource for practicing lucid dreaming. Keeping a dream journal entails routinely writing dreams and specifics like what was dreamed, feelings or sensations encountered, and any noteworthy symbols or themes. Individuals can document their progress in practicing lucid dreaming, recognize repeating themes and symbols, and gain insight into their dream patterns and inclinations by maintaining a dream journal. It may become more straightforward to identify when one dreams and becomes lucid due to this increasing self-awareness and insight into the dream realm.

To sum up, lucid dreaming activities include a range of methods and strategies for developing the capacity to become awake and conscious when dreaming. People can increase their chances of having lucid dreams and unlock the potential of their dream world for spiritual exploration, creativity, and personal growth by cultivating dream awareness, setting intentions, practicing wake-induced lucid dreaming (WILD), and keeping a dream journal.

Exploring the depths of the subconscious mind and using the power of the imagination to access life-changing experiences and insights into the nature of consciousness are made possible by lucid dreaming.

CHAPTER XIII

Shadow Work and Healing

Concept of Shadow Work

A healing process known as "shadow work" examines and integrates the unconscious parts of the psyche, sometimes known as the "shadow." The Swiss psychiatrist Carl Jung popularized the idea of the shadow, defining it as the unconscious side of the psyche that houses the aspects of the self that are suppressed, denied, or disowned. These shadow sides frequently show up as unwanted or destructive characteristics, feelings, or urges that we would rather keep to ourselves or from other people. To develop greater wholeness, authenticity, and self-acceptance, shadow work is bringing these hidden components of the self into conscious awareness, accepting them without passing judgment, and integrating them into the total self.

Shadow work is fundamentally about accepting and acknowledging the aspects of ourselves that we have denied, repressed, or discarded. This can be challenging and painful since it frequently calls for us to face parts of ourselves that we may find embarrassing, sore, or challenging to acknowledge. But we may start to mend the scars of the past and take back the parts of ourselves that we have denied by shedding light on these shadow sides and bringing them into conscious awareness. Through this integration process, we can become more entire and integrated beings, ready to accept all facets of who we are with compassion and love.

What we resist endures is one of the fundamental tenets of shadow work. Parts of ourselves that we deny or repress tend to show up subconsciously, which can result in marital problems, emotional upheaval, and recurring behavioral patterns. We can begin to comprehend the underlying reasons for these patterns and treat them from the ground up by bringing these shadow elements into conscious consciousness through shadow work. This enables us to release ourselves from the shackles of unconscious training and consciously make decisions in line with our beliefs and goals.

The introspection and self-reflection process is a crucial component of shadow work. Examining the beliefs, anxieties, and traumas beneath the surface of conscious awareness and how they have shaped our emotions, ideas, and actions is a common task of shadow work. Through self-reflection, we can begin to comprehend the significance of the shadow aspects in our lives and understand their beginnings. This higher self-awareness enables us to take charge of our recovery and development. It allows us to deliberately choose how we wish to react to our shadow selves.

Forgiveness and self-compassion are other processes that are included in shadow work. Feelings of shame, remorse, or self-condemnation may surface as we explore and meet our shadow selves. However, self-compassion and forgiveness are necessary for natural healing to take place. Let's let go of the hold of self-judgment and welcome our shadow sides with love and compassion, allowing us to reach new heights of healing and transformation. We may let go of the past and move on with more clarity, purpose, and self-love as we go through this forgiveness process.

In the end, shadow work is a path of empowerment and self-discovery that can result in significant healing and change. We can retrieve the aspects of ourselves that we have denied and incorporate them into our entire selves by confronting and accepting our shadow selves. Through this process, we can develop into more genuine, kind, and influential people who can live more freely, joyfully, and fulfillingly. Although shadow work is not always straightforward, it is an essential and incredibly fulfilling step to increased self-awareness, wholeness, and spiritual development. We can uncover the psyche's hidden mysteries and realize our souls' actual profundity and beauty through shadow work.

Techniques for Inner Healing

In order to live fully and genuinely, we may need to explore and heal emotional, psychological, and spiritual traumas. This process of self-discovery and transformation is known as inner healing. A variety of methods and exercises can aid inner healing, each offering a special strategy for development and healing.

Mindfulness meditation is a potent method for promoting inner healing. It entails developing an accepting and peaceful inner space and bringing conscious awareness to the current moment, thoughts, feelings, and sensations without passing judgment. Regular mindfulness meditation can increase emotional resiliency, compassion for others, and self-awareness. With this elevated state of awareness, greater insight and healing can result from exposing underlying emotional scars and behavioral patterns.

Breathwork is another helpful method for inner healing. Using deliberate breathing practices, breathwork helps the body eliminate emotional blockages, tension, and stress. Through mindfulness and deep breathing, people can unlock more profound levels of awareness and aid in discharging trauma and repressed emotions. Breathwork is a potent technique for facilitating emotional healing and balance and cleaning the body's energetic channels.

Another helpful method for inner healing is journaling. Writing down ideas, emotions, and experiences in a secure and encouraging setting is the practice of journaling. People can acquire clarity and insight into their inner world by writing down their thoughts and feelings and letting them run without restraint. This can help them identify unconscious patterns, beliefs, and emotions that could be causing them pain or suffering. In addition to offering a sense of catharsis and release, journaling can be helpful in processing and releasing challenging emotions.

Another effective method for healing oneself on the inside is creative expression. Indulging in artistic endeavors like writing, music, dance, or painting can assist people in connecting with their inner knowledge and expressing feelings that they find hard to put into words. Through artistic expression, people can profoundly and transformatively connect with their innermost selves, explore and release pent-up emotions, and access deeper insight and intuition.

Energy healing techniques like EFT (Emotional Freedom Techniques), Reiki, and acupuncture can also be helpful instruments for inner healing. These techniques support harmony, balance, and healing on a physical, emotional, and spiritual level by interacting with the body's subtle energy systems. By releasing emotional blockages, clearing stagnant energy, and restoring flow to the body's energy pathways, energy healing can help people release trauma, reduce stress, and cultivate a sense of well-being and wholeness.

Visualization and guided imagery are potent methods for inner healing. They use their imagination to create uplifting mental images and scenarios encouraging healing and transformation. Visualizing oneself as a whole, well, and healthy allows people to rewire their subconscious thoughts and develop a growth-promoting, optimistic outlook. By picturing oneself in a secure and encouraging setting and processing challenging feelings and experiences, guided imagery can also investigate and heal internal wounds, such as old traumas or unfavorable beliefs.

Lastly, connecting with nature can be a very effective method for inner healing. People can connect with their innermost selves and the earth's natural rhythms by spending time in nature, whether by trekking in the mountains, strolling along the beach, or just relaxing under a tree. We are grounded and centered by nature, which constantly reminds us of our connection to all other living things and the universe. People can discover comfort, calm, and spiritual healing by spending time in nature's stunning and serene surroundings.

In summary, inner healing is complex and demands bravery, dedication, and self-awareness. People can unleash their potential for significant change and development by integrating methods like guided imagery, breathwork, journaling, creative expression, energy healing, mindfulness meditation, guided imagery, and connecting with nature into their healing process. Each approach has a unique healing strategy and can be tailored to the person's requirements and preferences. If people are dedicated to their inner healing, they can recover their power, mend their wounds, and lead happier, more satisfying lives.

Integrating Shadow Aspects

Integrating "shadow" elements entails accepting, recognizing, and incorporating the unconscious parts of the psyche known as the "shadow." This is a transforming process. Carl Jung, a Swiss psychiatrist, popularized the idea of the shadow by defining it as the repressed, denied, or disowned elements of the self that contain undesirable or unpleasant features, feelings, and impulses. These shadow sides appear as thought patterns, emotional states, or behavioral patterns we want to keep hidden from ourselves and others. Trauma, early experiences, or social conditioning frequently bring them on. Greater wholeness, authenticity, and self-acceptance can only be attained by integrating shadow components, which call for bravery, self-awareness, and inner labor.

Being conscious of shadow characteristics is one of the first steps towards integrating them. This entails shedding light on our unconscious selves and accepting the ideas, emotions, and actions we may have been repressing or avoiding. This can be a difficult and painful process since it calls for us to face parts of ourselves that we might find embarrassing, sore, or challenging to acknowledge. But by bringing these shadow sides into conscious consciousness, we may start to comprehend where they came from and how they influence our lives.

Accepting our shadow selves without passing judgment is the next step after realizing who we are. Acceptance is recognizing these qualities as a natural part of the human experience, not endorsing or condoning them. Realizing that everyone has shadow sides is crucial since they are an inherent and necessary feature of being human. By embracing our shadow selves with empathy and understanding, we may start letting go of the guilt and self-criticism that could prevent us from completely incorporating them into our lives.

Bringing our shadow selves into conscious consciousness and integrating them into the whole self is the process of integration. To complete this process, we must investigate the traumas, phobias, and underlying beliefs that underlie our shadow selves and consider how they have shaped our attitudes, sentiments, and actions. We can start comprehending these unconscious patterns' origins and their role in influencing our lives by shedding light on them and bringing them into conscious consciousness. This higher self-awareness enables us to take charge of our recovery and development. It allows us to deliberately choose how we wish to react to our shadow selves.

Shadow work is one way to incorporate shadow characteristics. Working with the shadow through various therapeutic methods and approaches, including dream analysis, journaling, therapy, and creative expression, is known as shadow work. Through shadow work, people can discover and work through the underlying traumas, anxieties, and beliefs affecting their lives. They can also learn to accept and integrate their shadow selves with kindness and love. People can reclaim the aspects of themselves that they have rejected and incorporate them into their overall identity through this process of self-discovery and healing, which promotes greater wholeness, authenticity, and self-acceptance.

Through introspection and self-reflection, shadow features can also be integrated. Honest and open reflection on our thoughts, feelings, and behaviors can help us identify the unconscious patterns and ideas underlying our shadow selves. Being self-aware enables us to see the areas in which we might not be truly aligned with who we are and to take action to bring ourselves back into line with our goals and values. By using introspection, we can start to identify how our shadow selves are impacting our existence and consciously choose to bring them into awareness.

In summary, integrating shadow elements is a robust and transforming process that calls for introspection, bravery, and self-awareness. We can reclaim the parts we have disowned and attain more completeness, authenticity, and self-acceptance by recognizing, accepting, and integrating our shadow aspects. We can live more fully and authentically through this integration process, accepting all facets of who we are with compassion and love. We can create a life that aligns with ourselves and unleash the potential for profound healing and transformation by engaging in shadow work, self-reflection, and introspection.

CHAPTER XIV

Mystical Symbols and Correspondences

Understanding Symbolism

Since ancient times, symbols have been integral to human culture and spirituality, providing a channel for expression, communication, and spiritual connection with the divine. Rich levels of meaning and importance are inherent in mythical symbols, frequently representing spiritual principles, archetypal energies, and universal truths that cut across time and society. Gaining a grasp of symbolism is crucial for exploring the mystical worlds because it enables people to decipher the messages and hidden meanings inscribed in symbols and gain access to deeper levels of comprehension.

Symbolism is a soul language that speaks through patterns, archetypes, and images. Symbols communicate with us subconsciously, reaching beyond reason and into the more profound levels of awareness. They arouse feelings, pique curiosity, and provide intuitive insights to guide us through life's enigmas and foster a closer relationship with God. Symbols, whether they are conveyed through old sacred writings, myths, or religious imagery, act as a doorway to otherworldly domains, beckoning us to investigate the secret domains of the mind and the universe.

Knowing that symbols are multidimensional and can have several levels of significance is one of the fundamental concepts of symbolism. Symbols frequently function literally and symbolically, denoting more profound spiritual secrets and truths as well as actual objects or notions. For instance, the lotus flower, which stands for enlightenment, purity, and spiritual rebirth, is a widely used symbol in many spiritual traditions. The lotus flower symbolizes the possibility of spiritual development and transformation and the soul's journey from darkness to light. On a literal level, it is a stunning aquatic plant that blooms in murky waters.

Recognizing the idea of correspondences is a crucial component of comprehending symbols. Correspondences describe the connections and relationships between various symbols, components, and energies in the mystical and spiritual domains. For instance, there are correspondences in many esoteric traditions between the four cardinal directions (north, east, south, and west) and the elements (earth, air, fire, and water) and between astrological signs, colors, and numbers. By comprehending these correspondences, People can understand the universe's basic patterns and the interconnectivity of all things.

Another significant component of symbolism is archetypes, which stand for common themes and patterns in the collective unconscious. Archetypes include the trickster, the mother, the lover, the hero, and the wise old sage. They are symbolic depictions of basic human feelings and experiences. The world's myths, legends, and stories serve as potent symbols that speak to the most essential parts of the human psyche, expressing these archetypal energies. People can learn more about the universal forces shaping their lives and inner workings by comprehending archetypal symbology.

Another intriguing facet of mystical symbolism is sacred geometry, which symbolizes the fundamental mathematical ideas that underpin the universe's structure. Sacred geometric forms, which include the square, triangle, spiral, and circle, are present in nature and art and are said to have deep spiritual meaning.

These geometric shapes are believed to be gateways to higher awareness and divine understanding, embodying universal truths and energy. Through the study of sacred geometry, people can develop a greater sense of spiritual knowledge and connection and acquire insight into the fundamental harmony and order of the universe.

Finally, one must have a solid understanding of symbols to navigate the mystical realms and reach more profound insight and comprehension. Symbols convey universal truths and archetypal energies that cut beyond space and time, acting as portals to the subconscious and the divine. A person can achieve profound spiritual insight and transformation and uncover the hidden meanings and messages embedded within mystical symbols by realizing the multidimensional nature of symbols, comprehending correspondences, investigating archetypes, and studying sacred geometry. We can connect with the darkest recesses of our souls and the secrets of the cosmos through the language of symbolism, coming to appreciate the wonder and beauty of the mystical trip.

Using Correspondences in Rituals

In many spiritual and mystical traditions, correspondences—the relationships between disparate symbols, materials, and energies—are central to ritual practice. By comprehending and applying correspondences, practitioners can improve the potency and efficacy of their rituals by coordinating them with particular goals, energies, and spiritual concepts. Using correspondences in rituals, whether with planets, elements, colors, medicines, or other symbolic representations, can strengthen spiritual bonds, magnify intentions, and promote life-changing experiences.

Correspondences are frequently used in rituals by aligning components with particular directions. In various traditions, every direction is connected to a specific element: the north is connected to earth, the east to air, the south to fire, and the west to water. Practitioners can create sacred space and call upon the energies associated with each direction by incorporating these elemental correspondences into their ritual practice, which promotes harmony, balance, and alignment with the natural world. For instance, practitioners may face north, the earthly direction, and use the stabilizing energies of the earth element to support their aims during a ceremony for anchoring and stability.

Another potent correlation that ritualists utilize to invoke particular energies and intentions is color. Because every color has unique properties and vibrations, practitioners can align with corresponding energies and magnify their objectives by using specific colors in rituals. Red, for instance, is frequently linked to enthusiasm, energy, and movement, whereas blue is related to calmness, peace, and communication. Practitioners can increase the energetic potency of their rituals and create a visual depiction of their desired outcomes by selecting colors that align with their objectives.

Plants and herbs are frequently employed as correspondences in ceremonial practice; each herb has unique characteristics and connotations. Incorporating plants into rituals by burning, smudging, or making herbal sachets, practitioners can choose herbs that correspond with their aims, such as lavender for relaxation and cleansing or rosemary for protection and clarity. By utilizing these plant friends' energies, practitioners can strengthen their bond with the natural world and improve the efficacy of their rituals.

An additional helpful resource for coordinating rituals with specific cosmic energy and influences is planetary correspondences. By using planetary correspondences, practitioners can access the various qualities and archetypal energies each planet is linked to, enabling them to assist their intentions and objectives. For instance, rituals conducted at a full moon can center around manifestation, abundance, and release in line with the lunar cycle's expanding energies. Mercury is an introspective planetary influence. Therefore, rituals conducted during a retrograde may center on introspection, contemplation, and communication.

Another correspondence employed in ritual practice to access the vibrations and symbolic meanings connected with numbers is numerology. Practitioners can use numerological correspondences to communicate with particular energetic frequencies and intensify their intents, as each number carries distinct qualities and energies. For instance, the number seven is connected to spirituality, inner wisdom, and intuition, while the number three is frequently linked to creativity, expression, and communication. Practitioners can improve their rituals and strengthen their connection to the symbolic language of numbers by utilizing numerological correspondences.

To sum up, the potency and efficacy of spiritual practices can be increased by aligning intentions with particular energies and principles by using correspondences in rituals. By integrating correspondences into rituals, practitioners can strengthen their bond with the natural world, harmonize with cosmic energies, and magnify their objectives, regardless of whether they deal with elements, colors, herbs, planets, or numerology. Through correspondence, practitioners can establish sacred spaces, call forth specific energies, and lead people through life-changing experiences promoting spiritual development.

Crafting Personalized Symbols

For thousands of years, people have utilized symbols to express themselves, communicate with the holy, and connect. Although many symbols have cross-cultural and cross-traditional connotations, there is also immense value in creating customized symbols that speak directly to personal experiences, convictions, and goals. By creating individualized symbols, people may give their crafts a deeper, more meaningful meaning, which makes them powerful tools for spiritual development, self-expression, and empowerment.

One of the main advantages of creating personalized symbols is the adeptness to express oneself and be creative. People can use their experiences, convictions, and feelings to influence the design and meaning of a personalized symbol they create. Self-expression can be an uplifting and cathartic practice that helps people concretely externalize their deepest feelings and thoughts. Making customized symbols, whether sketching, painting, sculpting, or using other artistic mediums, offers a healing and transforming way to express oneself.

Creating customized symbols also enables people to access their inner wisdom and intuition. Symbols frequently emerge as significant pictures, shapes, or patterns from the subconscious mind. By connecting with their inner guidance system and letting symbols emerge organically, people can gain a greater awareness of who they are and what has happened to them. These customized symbols act as doorways to the subconscious, giving access to inner knowledge and secret realities that might not be reachable by reason alone.

Making customized symbols also offers the chance for self-discovery and empowerment. Customized symbols are potent instruments for self-discovery and empowerment because they are incredibly intimate and represent unique experiences, convictions, and goals. By designing symbols that speak to their own particular path, people can declare their identities in the world and reaffirm their values, beliefs, and objectives. Self-affirmation can be a freeing and inspiring process that enables people to live more purposefully and clearly and to accept their authenticity.

Creating individualized symbols also encourages a closer relationship with the spiritual and divine worlds. Historically, people have utilized symbols to invoke spiritual blessings and energies and to establish a connection with the divine. Customized symbols that align with one's spiritual practices and beliefs open powerful avenues for inspiration and sacred connection. These individualized symbols work as pillars for spiritual practice, offering a concrete conduit to the holy and enabling communication with higher states of awareness.

Personalized symbols have practical uses in daily life in addition to their spiritual importance. Personalized symbols can be used in daily routines and rituals to enhance personal growth and well-being, whether as protective talismans, aids for meditation and contemplation, or reminders of individual objectives and intentions. People can create surroundings filled with meaning and intention, promoting purpose and unity with their deepest wants and beliefs by adding personalized symbols to commonplace things and spaces.

Creating customized symbols is an intense and transforming activity that enables people to declare their identity and ideals, connect with the divine, express themselves artistically, and access their intuition and inner wisdom. Making customized symbols, whether by sketching, painting, sculpting, or using other artistic mediums, offers a way to express oneself that is very intimate and representative of one's experiences and convictions. People can use symbols to promote spiritual development, self-empowerment, and personal growth by imbuing their works with meaning and importance. By developing individualized symbols, people can open themselves up to profound self-discovery and development, strengthening their bonds with the divine, the world, and themselves.

CHAPTER XV

Daily Spiritual Practices

Creating a Daily Ritual

Our daily spiritual practices depend on maintaining our relationship with the divine, developing inner serenity, and promoting spiritual development. When we integrate daily rituals into our lives, we establish sacred times of introspection, prayer, and mindfulness that ground us in the here and now and bring us into alignment with our best selves. Establishing a daily ritual is a deeply personal and deliberate act that enables us to foster a feeling of meaning, connection, and purpose.

One of the main advantages of establishing a daily habit is the chance to focus and ground oneself. It's simple to get overwhelmed and cut off from ourselves and the outside world in the daily craziness of life. Daily rituals give us a sacred place to center and ground ourselves, allowing us to take a moment to breathe and reconnect with our innermost selves. Daily rituals, whether they involve prayer, meditation, or mindfulness exercises, assist us in grounding ourselves in the here and now and developing a sense of inner stability and serenity that enables us to face the day's challenges.

Regular rituals are also a potent way to nourish the soul and practice self-care. Making time for self-expression, self-reflection, and self-care amid our hectic lives is crucial. Everyday rituals provide a time and place set apart for fostering our mental, emotional, and physical health, enabling us to refuel our bodies and minds. Whether they involve writing, artistic endeavors, or time spent in nature, daily rituals offer a chance for self-nourishment and regeneration, crucial for preserving harmony and balance in our lives.

Establishing a routine also enables us to foster a closer relationship with the spiritual and divine worlds. Daily rituals allow us to connect with higher spiritual principles and access the wisdom and guidance of the holy, bridging the gap between the sacred and the commonplace. Daily practices help us tune into the rhythms of the cosmos and develop a sense of admiration, wonder, and reverence for the mysteries of creation. These practices can take many different forms, such as prayer, meditation, or ceremonies honoring the cycles of nature.

Daily rituals also help us to cultivate appreciation and thankfulness for all the blessings in our lives. It's critical to develop gratitude and an appreciation for the abundance and beauty around us, even in the face of life's obstacles and tribulations. Daily routines allow one to express gratitude through contemplation, prayer, or deeds of service and kindness. We may change our mindset from need and scarcity to abundance and thankfulness by developing a daily practice of appreciation. This will help us draw more blessings into our lives and feel more content and joyful.

Daily rituals also present a chance for development and transformation on a personal level. By making a daily practice commitment, we open up space for growth and evolution and develop self-awareness, discipline, and resilience. Daily rituals offer a space for intention-setting, goal-reflection on our values and objectives, and inspired action toward our desires. We may develop new behaviors and ways of being that align with our best selves by practicing consistently, enabling us to reach our full potential and lead more authentic and purposeful lives.

In summary, developing a daily ritual is a potent and transforming exercise that strengthens our relationship with the divine, develops inner calm, and promotes spiritual development. Daily rituals offer a sense of rootedness and centering, self-nurturing and care, spiritual connection, appreciation and thankfulness, personal growth, and metamorphosis. Adhering to a routine establishes a hallowed framework for spiritual growth, enabling us to harmonize with our ultimate identities and lead more meaningful, connected lives.

Maintaining Spiritual Balance

Keeping our spiritual equilibrium amid life's obstacles, obligations, and diversions is crucial to our well-being and inner peace. Spiritual balance is a condition of equilibrium in which we are in sync with the cycles of the universe, connected to our inner selves, and in line with our aims and ideals. It entails fostering our mental, emotional, spiritual, and physical selves to bring about a sense of integration and wholeness.

To keep spirituality in balance, developing self-awareness and mindfulness is essential. By tuning into our thoughts, feelings, and sensations with curiosity and without passing judgment, we can become more aware of our inner world and the minute fluctuations in our energy and state of being. Through mindfulness exercises like body awareness, breathwork, and meditation, we may strengthen our inner connection and improve present-moment awareness, which will help us deal more calmly and clearly with life's ups and downs.

Nurturing our relationship with the divine or higher power is crucial to keeping spiritual balance. Establishing a connection with the divine, whether by prayer, meditation, ritual, or spending time in nature, offers us a source of courage, direction, and support. We can find comfort and tranquility in the face of life's uncertainties and difficulties by giving ourselves to a higher power and believing in our divine wisdom and timing of the universe.

This allows us to know that we are held and supported by a force that is bigger than ourselves.

Choosing and acting in a way consistent with our aims and ideals is another way we might preserve spiritual equilibrium. Living by our core beliefs and goals gives us a sense of unity and integrity that promotes inner peace and contentment. Setting limits, declining obligations or pursuits that sap our energy, and prioritizing pursuits that uplift our spirits and serve our purpose are a few examples of how to do this. When we act out our values and objectives, we establish a sense of coherence and alignment that promotes our well-being and spiritual development.

Additionally, looking after our physical, emotional, and mental well-being is necessary to preserve spiritual harmony. Our general health and energy are closely linked to our spiritual well-being; neglecting any of these areas can knock us off balance. Maintaining our physical well-being requires us to follow specific guidelines, such as managing stress, eating healthfully, sleeping, and exercising frequently. Similarly, taking care of our emotional and mental well-being through counseling, writing, and creative expression enables us to process and let go of challenging feelings, build resilience, and promote inner clarity and serenity.

Moreover, developing an attitude of appreciation and thankfulness for the blessings in our lives is essential to preserving spiritual balance. Practicing gratitude is a powerful way to invite greater richness and joy into our lives by shifting our attention from what we lack to what we have. By setting aside time each day to recognize and appreciate the benefits that surround us, we can nurture a sense of fulfillment and contentment that nourishes our souls and facilitates our spiritual growth.

Preserving spiritual equilibrium is critical to our general health and sense of inner peace. It entails developing mindfulness and self-awareness, strengthening our relationship with the divine, ensuring that our deeds reflect our values and goals, looking after our bodily, mental, and emotional well-being, and developing an attitude of thankfulness and appreciation for all the benefits in our lives. We build a foundation of spiritual balance by integrating these practices into our daily lives, enhancing our general well-being and enabling us to face life's obstacles with grace and grit.

Journaling and Reflection

Reflection and journaling are practical tools for fostering personal development, self-awareness, and inner growth. By writing down our reflections, we establish a sacred space where we can honestly and authentically explore our ideas, feelings, and experiences. Writing in a journal helps us become more self-aware, clarify our goals and ideals, and strengthen our bond with our inner selves.

The potential of journaling to offer a secure and accepting environment for self-expression is one of its main advantages. We can intentionally explore our thoughts and feelings in a notebook without worrying about being judged or criticized. This freedom enables us to explore the depths of our subconscious and reveal wants, aspirations, and hidden truths that might be lying there. We can facilitate emotional release and catharsis, get insight into our inner workings, and let go of pent-up emotions by giving voice to our deepest thoughts and feelings.

Additionally, journaling is a valuable technique for developing perspective and clarity about life's difficulties and problems. Writing in a journal enables us to take a step back from the jumble of our thoughts and obtain an S-eye view of the issue when faced with tough choices or uncertainty. Writing allows us to examine several viewpoints, balance advantages and disadvantages, and understand the underlying motives and anxieties that might guide our decisions. We may make well-informed decisions consistent with our beliefs and goals when we engage in introspection and reflection, enhancing our sense of contentment and authenticity in life.

Furthermore, journaling is an effective method for monitoring our development and evolution throughout time. We produce a physical documentation of our life's journey by writing down our ideas, emotions, and experiences in a journal. We can monitor our development, recognize our accomplishments, and grow from our failures thanks to this record. When we review our earlier entries, we can see trends, themes, and revelations that show the course of our development. This knowledge may be inspiring because it serves as a reminder of our progress and an incentive to continue toward personal growth.

Journaling is also a valuable tool for goal-setting and achievement. We can make our intentions clear and resolve to act toward our goals and dreams by submitting them to a paper in a journal. By keeping a journal, we may track our progress, celebrate our victories, and break down our goals into small chunks. Additionally, journaling gives us a place to consider our achievements and failures, draw lessons from them, and change course as necessary. Setting goals and reflecting on our lives allows us to live more intentionally, purposefully, and in line with our deepest desires.

Additionally, journaling can be a very effective way to work through challenging feelings and situations. A secure and encouraging way to express our emotions and make sense of our experiences during difficulties, traumas, or emotional upheavals is through journaling. We can get perspective on our challenges, investigate our feelings' underlying reasons and meanings, and find comfort and healing through self-expression through writing. By keeping a journal, we can learn about our inner selves, let go of suppressed emotions, and develop inner serenity and fortitude in the face of hardship.

Journaling and introspection are practical tools for fostering personal development, self-awareness, and transformation. Journaling helps us become more self-aware, gain insight into our inner workings, and develop a stronger connection to our inner selves by providing a sacred space for self-expression, gaining clarity and perspective, tracking our personal growth, setting and achieving goals, and processing difficult emotions and experiences. We can face life's obstacles with grace and resiliency, live more authentically and purposefully, and set out on a path of self-discovery and personal development that results in increased fulfillment by journaling regularly.

CHAPTER XVI

Community and Solitary Practice

Benefits of Coven Membership

In Wicca and other paganism, practitioners can choose to work alone or as part of a coven, a group of people who share similar beliefs and gather to worship, learn, and perform magic. While solitary and coven practices both have special merits, there are a number of perks associated with coven participation that can further one's spiritual development and strengthen one's bond with the craft.

One of coven membership's main advantages is the sense of belonging and community it offers. Since humans are naturally social beings, having a community of like-minded practitioners can be very consoling and enlightening. Members of a coven gather to observe rituals, share information and wisdom, celebrate the Sabbats and Esbats, and assist one another on their spiritual journeys. This companionship encourages a sense of connection and belonging that can be challenging to obtain in solo practice. It also serves as a source of inspiration and support for spiritual development.

Furthermore, coven membership provides chances for education and spiritual growth that might not be possible in solo practice. Members of a coven can benefit from each other's aggregate knowledge and experience, as well as the direction and mentoring of more seasoned witches and priests/priestesses. This educational setting offers a safe place for questioning, experience sharing, and getting advice from other travelers on the road. It also enables individuals to understand better Wiccan theology, ritual practices, magical skills, and spiritual concepts.

Membership in a coven also allows one to participate in collective rituals and ceremonies, which can be incredibly inspiring and transformational. Rituals are generally carried out in a coven setting with a great degree of intention, focus, and intensity, and the group's combined efforts can increase the potency of magical operations and spiritual pursuits. By participating in rituals in groups, people can feel a sense of connectedness and communal energy that can strengthen their magical skills and expand their spiritual experiences. Group rituals also offer chances for collective worship, celebration, and adoration of the divine, which cultivates awe, wonder, and reverence for life's mysteries.

Additionally, coven participation provides chances for community service and leadership. Members of many covens can assume leadership positions, such as High Priest, High Priestess, or Ritual Facilitator, which enables them to offer their abilities, knowledge, and skills to the community. In addition to providing chances for spiritual development, self-discovery, and personal growth, leadership positions within covens allow practitioners to influence the lives of other practitioners positively. Coven membership frequently includes involvement in service projects, community outreach, and charitable endeavors to enable members to contribute to their communities and change the world.

In conclusion, coven membership gives several benefits that can enhance one's spiritual path and strengthen their bond with the craft, even if both solitary and coven practice offer distinct advantages. Coven membership provides a supportive and enriching environment for people to explore their spirituality, strengthen their connection to the divine, and develop as craft practitioners. It does this by offering community and belonging, learning and spiritual development opportunities, participation in group rituals and ceremonies, and leadership and service opportunities within the community. The path of Wicca offers chances for spiritual progression, self-discovery, and personal growth that can profoundly and meaningfully impact one's life, whether practiced alone or in a coven.

Practices for Solitary Wiccans

For many practitioners of Wicca, solitary practice is a deeply personal and fulfilling path that allows for individual exploration, self-discovery, and spiritual growth. While covens offer a sense of community and shared experience, solitary Wiccans can forge a unique connection to the divine, explore their spiritual path, and deepen their understanding of the craft in their own time and at their own pace. Solitary practice offers a myriad of practices and rituals that can be tailored to fit each practitioner's individual needs and preferences, allowing for a deeply personal and authentic spiritual journey.

One of the foundational practices for solitary Wiccans is the observation of the Sabbats and Esbats, which are the sacred festivals and lunar celebrations that mark the cycles of the natural world. These observances provide opportunities for solitary practitioners to connect with the rhythms of nature, honor the changing seasons, and cultivate a deeper connection to the earth and its cycles. Whether through simple rituals performed in the privacy of one's home or outdoor ceremonies conducted in nature, observing the Sabbats and Esbats allows solitary. Wiccans can cultivate awe, wonder, and reverence for life's mysteries by connecting with the planet's energies and the universe.

Another essential practice for solitary Wiccans is meditation and visualization, which allows practitioners to quiet the mind, center themselves, and connect with their inner selves and the divine. Solitary Wiccans can cultivate inner peace, clarity, and presence through regular meditation, authorizing them to access more profound insight and wisdom. Visualization techniques can focus the mind, manifest desires, and connect with spiritual energies and entities, allowing solitary practitioners to tap into their imagination's power and harness the universe's creative forces.

Furthermore, solitary Wiccans often create sacred spaces and perform rituals and spells to honor the divine, work magic, and manifest intentions. Whether through the casting of a circle, the invocation of deities, or the use of ritual tools and symbols, creating sacred space allows solitary practitioners to set the stage for their spiritual work and cultivate a sense of reverence and sanctity in their practice. Rituals and spells can be tailored to fit each practitioner's individual needs and intentions, allowing for a deeply personal and meaningful spiritual experience that resonates with the practitioner's unique journey and aspirations.

Moreover, solitary Wiccans often incorporate divination practices into their spiritual work, using tools such as tarot cards, runes, or scrying to gain insight into their lives, receive guidance from the divine, and explore the mysteries of the universe. Divination allows solitary practitioners to tap into their intuition, access more profound levels of wisdom, and gain clarity about their path and purpose. Whether through daily card pulls, complete moon readings, or ceremonial divination rituals, divination practices provide a bond with the divine and receive guidance and inspiration on the journey of self-discovery and spiritual growth.

In conclusion, solitary practice offers a rich and diverse array of practices and rituals that can nurture the inner flame of the solitary Wiccan. From observing the Sabbats and Esbats to meditation and visualization to the creation of sacred space and the performance of rituals and spells to the practice of divination, solitary Wiccans have a luxury of tools and techniques at their disposal for deepening their connection to the divine, exploring their spiritual path, and cultivating a sense of wonder, reverence, and awe for the mysteries of existence. Through regular practice and dedication to their craft, solitary Wiccans can embark on a journey of self-discovery and spiritual evolution that leads to greater fulfillment, authenticity, and alignment with their true selves.

Building a Supportive Spiritual Community

In Wicca and other pagan traditions, building a supportive spiritual community is essential for fostering connection, growth, and empowerment. A supportive spiritual community provides a shielded and nourished environment where individuals can share knowledge, experiences, and wisdom and support one another on their spiritual journey. Whether through joining a coven, attending rituals and gatherings, or participating in online forums and discussion groups, building a supportive spiritual community allows individuals to cultivate meaningful connections, deepen their understanding of the craft, and experience a sense of belonging and camaraderie that enriches their spiritual practice and enhances their overall well-being.

One of the primary benefits of building a supportive spiritual community is the opportunity for connection and fellowship with like-minded individuals. Humans are naturally gregarious creatures, and having a sympathetic community of fellow practitioners can be immensely comforting and enriching. In a spiritual community, individuals can connect with others who share their values, beliefs, and interests to form friendships and bonds that can last a lifetime. This sense of connection and belonging provides a source of encouragement, inspiration, and support that can help individuals navigate life's challenges and celebrate life's joys with grace and resilience.

Moreover, building a supportive spiritual community offers opportunities for learning and growth that may not be available in solitary practice. Within a community setting, individuals have access to the compiled knowledge and expertise of their fellow practitioners and the guidance and mentorship of more experienced witches and priests/priestesses. This learning environment allows individuals to deepen their understanding of Wiccan theology, ritual practices, magical techniques, and spiritual concepts, and it provides a supportive space for asking questions, sharing experiences, and receiving feedback and guidance from others on the path. By engaging with a supportive spiritual community, individuals can expand their knowledge, develop their skills, and grow as practitioners of the craft.

Furthermore, building a supportive spiritual community offers opportunities for participation in group rituals and ceremonies, which can be profoundly transformative and empowering experiences. In a community setting, rituals are often performed with a high level of intention, focus, and energy, and the group's combined efforts can amplify the effectiveness of magical workings and spiritual endeavors. Participating in group rituals allows individuals to experience a sense of collective energy and connection that can enhance their magical abilities and deepen their spiritual experiences. Group rituals also offer chances for collective worship, celebration, and adoration of the divine, which cultivates awe, wonder, and reverence for life's mysteries.

Additionally, building a supportive spiritual community provides opportunities for leadership and service within the community. In many spiritual communities, members can take on leadership roles, such as High Priestess, High Priest, or ritual facilitator, which allows them to bestow their skills, knowledge, and talents to the group. In addition to offering chances for spiritual development, self-discovery, and personal growth, leadership roles within a community also allow practitioners to influence the existence of other practitioners positively. Participating in service projects, community outreach, and charitable endeavors will enable members to give back to their communities and make a difference in the world.

In conclusion, building a supportive spiritual community is essential for nurturing connection, growth, and empowerment in Wicca and other pagan traditions. By providing a sense of connection and fellowship, opportunities for learning and development, participation in group rituals and ceremonies, and opportunities for leadership and service within the community, a supportive spiritual community enriches the lives of its members and enhances their spiritual practice and well-being. Whether through joining a coven, attending rituals and gatherings, or participating in online forums and discussion groups, building a supportive spiritual community allows people to meet others who share their interests, expand their comprehension of the craft, and experience the transformative power of community on their spiritual journey.

CHAPTER XVII

Living a Mystical Life

Integrating Wiccan Principles into Everyday Life

To live a mystical life is to live according to Wiccan ideals and principles in our thoughts, deeds, and interactions—not simply by doing rituals and casting spells. By applying Wiccan values to our everyday existence, we can live in harmony with one another, bloom a closer relationship with the divine, and respect the holiness of the natural world. We can change our lives and find more joy, fulfillment, and purpose by directing our thoughts, intentions, and deeds under Wiccan teachings.

Believing that everything is related is one of the core tenets of Wicca. Wiccans acknowledge that all living things in the cosmos are interrelated and dependent upon one another and that we are all a part of a more excellent web of life. Cultivating an awareness of this interconnectivity and respecting the holiness of all living things are essential components of leading a mystical life. This entails acknowledging the divinity inside us and others and treating people with kindness, compassion, and respect. We can develop a sense of oneness and unity with the cosmos and live in harmony with the divine flow of life by acknowledging the interconnectedness of all things.

The belief in the power of intention and manifestation is another fundamental tenet of Wicca. Wiccans hold that our ideas, intentions, and deeds can influence our reality. Using the power of intention to manifest our goals and bring about positive change in the world is a necessary part of leading a mystical life. This entails establishing specific intentions, coordinating our activities with our objectives, and having faith in the universe's divine timing and direction. By developing an intentional living practice, we may bring our goals and desires to life and design a life that aligns with our most significant potential.

Living a mystical life also means respecting nature's cycles and the seasons. Wiccans keep the Sabbats, which fall on the equinoxes, solstices, and other important dates in the calendar, to celebrate the changing seasons. We can honor the sanctity of the land, the cycles of birth, growth, death, and rebirth, and tune ourselves into the rhythms of the natural world when we live in harmony with the earth's natural cycles. We can develop a closer bond with the land and the natural environment and coexist peacefully with the seasons and life's cycles by respecting the cycles of nature.

Furthermore, cultivating presence and mindfulness in our day-to-day existence is a requirement of leading a mystical life. All parts of mindfulness are developing a sense of presence and awareness in our day-to-day experiences and remunerating attention to the present moment with openness, curiosity, and acceptance. We can build up our relationship with the divine and develop awe and thankfulness for the wonder and beauty of life by engaging in mindfulness practices. We may interact with life's experiences and find joy and fulfillment in the small pleasures of daily life when we live in the present.

In summary, leading a mystical life involves incorporating Wiccan ideals and concepts into our daily lives rather than merely performing rituals and spells. We can blossom a closer relationship with God and live more in line with our best potential by respecting the interconnection of all things, using intention and manifestation to their fullest, recognizing the cycles of nature, and engaging in mindfulness and presence practices. Living a mystical existence enables us to live in harmony with the natural world, ourselves, and others while experiencing greater joy, purpose, and fulfillment.

Mindfulness and Presence

The current world is fast-paced, making it tranquil to get caught up in the day-to-day grind and allow our thoughts to wander from one topic to the next. However, the demands and distractions of modern life can be effectively counterbalanced by mindfulness and presence, which helps us strengthen our sense of awareness and connection to the present moment.

The practice of mindfulness involves concentrating attention on the present moment with acceptance, curiosity, and openness. It means giving our thoughts, feelings, sensations, and surroundings our attention without attachment or judgment. Through mindfulness practice, we can strengthen our sense of clarity, attentiveness, and present-moment cognizance in our daily lives, allowing us to engage fully with the richness and beauty of each moment.

One of mindfulness's salient benefits is its ability to promote relaxation and reduce tension. By practicing mindfulness, we can increase our consciousness of the present moment, which allows us to stop thinking about the past or the future and focus just on the here and now. In the midst of life's obstacles, this can help foster a sense of serenity and tranquility and lessen emotions of overwhelm and anxiety.

Additionally, practicing mindfulness can improve our interpersonal interactions and communication. By being more mindful and present in our interactions, we can improve our ability to listen intently to others and empathize with their experiences. This can encourage a more vital empathy and compassion for other people and more profound understanding and connections in our interactions.

Additionally, practicing mindfulness can improve our general health and standard of living. By engaging in mindfulness practices, we can make deliberate decisions consistent with our aims and beliefs by escalating our awareness of our thoughts, feelings, and behaviors. This can support us in developing a stronger sense of authenticity, fulfillment, and purpose in our lives by enabling us to break free from unhelpful thought and behavior patterns.

The technique of being present and attentive in the here and now, free from distraction or obsession, is known as presence. Whether we're doing the dishes, going for a stroll in the park, or conversing with a loved one, it entails giving whatever we're doing our whole attention and presence. By practicing the present, we can fully enjoy and recognize the richness and beauty of life by feeling a stronger sense of connection and aliveness in our day-to-day experiences.

One of its main advantages is the capacity of presence to boost creativity and productivity. When we are totally present and involved in our tasks, we can reach a state of flow where our thoughts and actions are in harmony and effortless. This can help us reach our full potential and express ourselves more fully in the world by increasing inspiration, creativity, and efficiency in our work and creative efforts.

Furthermore, being present can strengthen our ties to the natural world and the sanctity of life. When we are present and attentive, we may appreciate the wonder and beauty of the world around us with open hearts and new eyes. This can help us develop a more profound feeling of respect and admiration for the tremendous mystery and enchantment of existence and the connectivity of all living things.

Practicing presence and mindfulness can help you develop awareness and connection daily. By giving the current moment our whole attention while remaining open, curious, and accepting, we may improve relationships, lessen stress, and foster a greater feeling of fulfillment and well-being. By practicing mindfulness and presence, whether formally or just by incorporating it into our everyday activities, we can experience more serenity, joy, and aliveness in every moment.

Continuous Spiritual Growth

A lifetime path of self-awareness, self-discovery, and self-improvement, continuous spiritual growth entails developing our growth, more significant comprehension of the cosmos, and strengthening our relationship with the divine. It's a constant discovery, learning, and transformation process that calls for commitment, purpose, and an open heart and mind. Constant spiritual development considers many facets of our lives, such as our values, relationships, daily routines, and beliefs. It develops gradually and iteratively as we work through life's ups and downs.

Introspection and self-reflection are crucial components of ongoing spiritual development. By pausing to reflect on our ideas, feelings, and experiences, we can learn more about ourselves, our motives, and our behavioral patterns. We can also find limiting ideas and phobias, pinpoint opportunities for improvement, and build a better knowledge of who we are and where we fit in the world. Practicing self-reflection techniques like writing, meditation, and contemplation helps us become more self-aware and advance spiritually.

Moreover, ongoing spiritual development necessitates a dedication to education and inquiry. This entails reading spiritual books, doctrines, and customs and looking for fresh insights and encounters that challenge and broaden our conceptions of God and the cosmos. We can extend our spiritual horizons and strengthen our bond with the boundless wisdom and mystery of existence by being receptive to new ideas, concepts, and beliefs. Furthermore, conversing and living in a community with other seekers enables us to exchange ideas, benefit from knowledge, and encourage one another on our spiritual paths.

Cultivating spiritual practices and rituals is another crucial component of ongoing spiritual development. Engaging in these practices can strengthen our relationship with the divine, become more in tune with our true selves, and reach higher awareness. Regular spiritual practice, whether meditation, prayer, chanting, or ceremonial magic, allows us to open our hearts, calm our minds, and become more sensitive to the universe's subtle energies. We can build a foundation for spiritual development and transformation by implementing these practices into our daily lives, which will help us face life's obstacles with grace and grit.

Furthermore, maintaining our commitment to life under our ideals and ideas is necessary for ongoing spiritual development. This entails developing qualities like love, compassion, honesty, and authenticity in our words, deeds, and thoughts. It also entails making deliberate decisions that respect the interdependence of all living things and our relationship with the almighty. We may create a meaningful, fulfilling, and purposeful life by living by our beliefs, and we can also benefit the earth and the human race as a whole.

Continuous spiritual development also necessitates a readiness to accept uncertainty and change. Leaving our comfort zones, facing our anxieties and uncertainties, and bravely and firmly facing the unknown are common steps toward personal growth. We may increase our capacity for love, pleasure, and abundance and have a greater sense of aliveness and vitality in our lives by the discomfort that comes with growth and change. Furthermore, by seeing obstacles and failures as chances for development and education, we can face life with fortitude and hope, understanding that each event can enhance and enrich our spiritual journey.

To sum up, lifelong spiritual growth is an ongoing process of self-awareness, self-discovery, and self-improvement. It entails introspection, education, discovery, and the development of spiritual rites and activities that strengthen our ties to the cosmos and the divine. Our spiritual growth path can be accelerated, and we can feel greater fulfillment, purpose, and joy in life by living by our values, accepting change and uncertainty, and keeping an open mind to new ideas and experiences.

CONCLUSION

In conclusion, "Wiccan Mysticism and Spirituality: Journeying into the Mystical Realm: Exploring Wiccan Spirituality and Mysticism" presents a comprehensive guide for those embarking on a journey of spiritual exploration within the Wiccan tradition. Throughout the pages of this book, readers have been invited to delve into the rich tapestry of Wiccan spirituality, uncovering the ancient wisdom, sacred practices, and mystical insights passed down through generations. From the origins and history of Wicca to the core beliefs and principles, from the celebration of the Sabbats to the practice of spellcraft and magick, each chapter has offered a window into the mystical realm of Wiccan spirituality.

As readers journey through these pages, they have been encouraged to deepen their connection to the divine, honor the sacredness of the natural world, and cultivate a sense of wonder, reverence, and awe for the mysteries of existence. Whether practicing alone or as part of a community, casting spells, or communing with nature spirits, the principles and practices outlined in this book provide a roadmap for spiritual growth, self-discovery, and personal transformation.

As the journey continues beyond the pages of this book, may readers carry with them the wisdom, insights, and inspiration they have gained. May they continue to explore the depths of Wiccan spirituality with an open heart and a curious mind. May they find guidance, support, and empowerment on their spiritual path and experience the magic and mystery of the Wiccan tradition in all aspects of their lives.